a taste of
NEWPORT

A guide to 15 of Newport's finest restaurants . . . plus
more than 100 of their most popular recipes.

by Gillian Drake

PUBLISHED BY SHANK PAINTER PUBLISHING COMPANY

Books in the "Taste of" series:

A TASTE OF BOSTON
A TASTE OF CAPE COD
A TASTE OF PROVINCETOWN
A TASTE OF NEWPORT
A TASTE OF PROVIDENCE

may be ordered from
Shank Painter Publishing Co.
650 Commercial St., Provincetown, MA 02657
(order form on page 95)

"A Taste of Newport"
conceived, written, designed and produced by Gillian Drake

© 1990, Gillian Drake

Printed in USA

Introduction

Restaurants are among Newport's finest assets; they're diverse in style and cover a broad range of tastes. This is not surprising, considering the rich cultural heritage of Newport. As one of America's most historic cities, Newport is steeped in Colonial and Gilded Age tradition, but the City by the Sea is at the same time vibrant, offering a cornucopia of diversions: music festivals, regattas, boat shows, tennis tournaments, mansions, museums, and beaches. Fortunately, Newport's restaurant scene admirably matches this vitality and tradition.

As you might expect from its seaside location, Newport is famous for great seafood. Narragansett Bay and the offshore waters produce a vast array of fish and shellfish: tuna, swordfish, bluefish, lobster, mussels, clams (steamers and quahogs) and much more. And since Newport is a fishing port, freshness is assured. The restaurants also offer a wide variety of locally-grown vegetables and meat, so you can freely sample the best the area has to offer.

Newport's restaurants run the historical and culinary gamut, as seen in the classic Colonial ambiance and fine cuisine of the Whitehorse Tavern and the Clarke Cooke House; in the turn-of-the-century elegance of the Canfield House and the Inn at Castle Hill; the salty flavor of the waterfront at the Pier; the funky atmosphere of ever-popular Salas'; the elegant contemporary cuisine of Le Bistro; the French country ambiance of La Petite Auberge; the convivial neighborhood spirit of Cafe Zelda and the Rhumbline; the authentic Italian cuisine at Sardella's; the excellent home-cooking at Muriel's; and the convivial pub atmosphere of Yesterday's and the Brick Alley Pub. You can dine on a deck and watch the sun set over a harbor full of yachts, or enjoy a quiet candle-lit dinner in a romantic setting, or maybe unwind in a lively cafe or neighborhood pub.

Most of Newport's restaurants are located in and around the waterfront area, so they are within walking distance from many hotels and inns. As you explore the city, you'll enjoy sampling the varied cuisine and ambiance offered by its restaurants. During the busy season, reservations are recommended where available. You may want to try the most popular restaurants on a weekday. The slower seasons (late fall, winter and early spring) are also great times to check out restaurants. Most are open year round and will appreciate your business during a more tranquil period.

If you're looking for great food in a unique setting, this is the place to be. Welcome to Newport, you'll love it here.

Terrence Gavan
Newport, Rhode Island
Author: *"The Complete Guide to Newport"*
and *"The Barons of Newport"*

Contents

Location of Restaurants

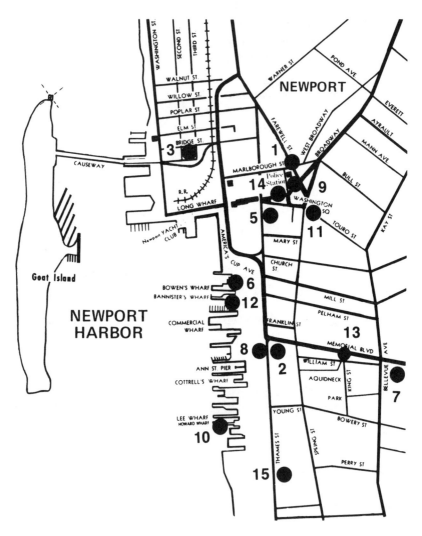

1. **White Horse Tavern** • page 8
    Marlborough & Farewell Streets. 849-3600

2. **The Ark** • page 14
    348 Thames Street. 849-3808.

3. **Rhumbline** • page 21
    62 Bridge Street. 849-6950.

4. **Inn at Castle Hill** • page 25
   Ocean Drive. 849-3800.

5. **Brick Alley Pub** • page 30
   140 Thames Street. 849-8291.

6. **Le Bistro** • page 36
   Bowen's Wharf. 849-7778.

7. **Canfield House** • page 43
   5 Memorial Boulevard. 847-0416.

8. **Salas'** • page 49
   341 Thames Street. 846-8772.

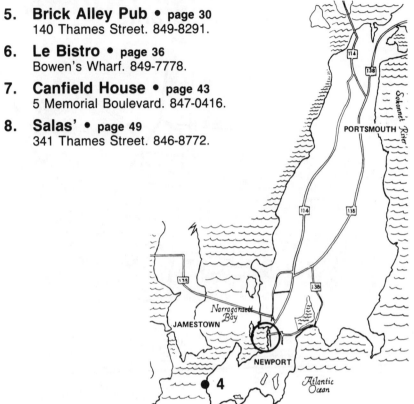

9. **La Petite Auberge** • page 54
   19 Charles Street. 849-6669.

10. **The Pier** • page 59
    West Howard Wharf. 849-3100.

11. **Muriel's** • page 65
    Corner of Spring & Touro Streets. 849-7780.

12. **Clarke Cooke House** • page 70
    Bannister's Wharf. 849-2900.

13. **Sardella's** • page 78
    30 Memorial Boulevard. 849-6312.

14. **Yesterday's** • page 82
    28 Washington Square. 847-0116.

15. **Cafe Zelda** • page 87
    528 Thames Street. 849-4002.

WHITE HORSE TAVERN

The **White Horse Tavern** has been providing New Englanders with food and spirits since 1687 and is the oldest operating tavern in the country. This historic building was constructed some time in the mid 1600s as the two-room, two-story residence of Francis Brinley. William Mayes, Sr., bought the building in 1673 and obtained a tavern license in 1687. As a tavern, the building continued a very colorful history, being used also as a court room and meeting place for the Colonial Legislature. The Nichols family took over the operation of the tavern in the early 1700s and the building remained in the family for two centuries until 1901 when it was sold and turned into a boarding house. Neglected and moldering, it was acquired by the Preservation Society of Newport who restored the venerable building and opened it as a restaurant in 1957.

Painted Colonial red, the exterior of the Tavern epitomizes 18th century Newport architecture with its gambrel roof, clapboard walls and pedimented doors bordering the sidewalk. Inside, exemplifying 17th century design, are massive summer beams, wide polished floorboards and cavernous brick fireplaces. The building has been restored with a great amount of attention to detail and authentic 17th century antiques help recreate the atmosphere of times gone by. In the dining room, Windsor style chairs, Colonial print curtains and tables set with flickering candles, fine crystal, and white table linens create a comfortable yet elegant setting for fine dining.

Now privately owned, the White Horse Tavern continues a 300 year tradition of hospitality. Featuring a continental menu adapted to New England ingredients and an abundance of fresh grown herbs, the White Horse Tavern is now noted for fine dining. Entree specialties include Lobster White Horse Tavern, individual Beef Wellington, and roasted rack of lamb, and appetizers include Tavern Gravlax and wild mushroom ratatouille. The White Horse Tavern also offers over 400 different varieties in its extensive wine program. Noted yearly by the Wine Spectator, the tavern was given an Award of Excellence for the variety of wines offered to its customers. Assisted by professional wine stewards, the White Horse Tavern combines fine food and wine with the most gracious of service.

WHITE HORSE TAVERN

Corner of Marlborough & Farewell Streets, Newport • (401) 849-3600

OPEN: 12 noon to 10 pm, seven days a week, all year
LUNCH: 12 noon to 3 pm (closed for lunch on Tuesday)
DINNER: 6 to 10 pm
SUNDAY BRUNCH: 12 noon to 3 pm
SEATS: 134
SEPARATE BAR: Open 12 noon to 1:00 am
CHILDREN'S PORTIONS: not served
CREDIT CARDS: all major credit card accepted
PARKING: private lot
RESERVATIONS: advised, call 849-3600

White Horse Salad Dressing   SERVES 6-8

1 egg
⅓ cup raspberry vinegar
1 tablespoon whole-grain mustard
1 quart salad oil

⅓ cup raspberry vinegar
⅔ cup heavy cream
chopped fresh dill
salt and pepper

Whisk together egg, ⅓ cup vinegar and mustard. Slowly whisk in salad oil. Stir in the other ⅓ cup of vinegar and the heavy cream, being careful not to break the emulsion. Add fresh chopped dill and salt and pepper to taste.

Five-Mushroom Ratatouille SERVES 6-8

1 lb. butter
bunch parsley, chopped
2 cloves garlic
3 lemons
1 oz. Pernod
12 oz. button mushrooms
6 oz. French morelles
6 oz. French cepes
6 oz. French chanterelles
6 oz. black Chinese mushrooms
10 oz. heavy cream
10 oz. veal demi glace
16 slices white bread

Soften butter, chop parsley fine, crush garlic, and make lemon juice from lemons. Clean and quarter mushrooms, removing stems. Combine butter, garlic, parsley, Pernod, pepper and salt to form garlic butter. This can be done manually. Saute all the mushrooms in garlic butter until about three-quarters cooked. Add the veal demi glace and heavy cream, bring to a boil and let reduce to a combined sauce. Finish with a splash of lemon juice.

To make the croutons: cut bread in desired shapes (we use heart shapes) and saute in butter, in a separate pan, until crisp and brown. Serve garnished with croutons and chopped parsley.

Poached Oysters in Puff Pastry with Saffron Cream Sauce SERVES 4

20 freshly-shucked oysters
10 oz. fresh spinach, blanched, drained and chopped
4 oz. garlic butter
1½'' rounds of puff pastry, baked (one per oyster)
a little beurre rouge and beurre blanc
chopped parsley and fresh dill to garnish
4 oz. Pernod
½ teaspoon saffron
1 quart heavy cream

To make the sauce: reduce Pernod by half, add saffron and cream and reduce again to 3 cups. Season with salt and pepper and keep warm.

Court Bouillon:
2 cups cry Vermouth
2 cups water
¼ teaspoon black peppercorns
1 stalk of celery, chopped
1 leek, chopped

Boil all ingredients in a stockpot for 20 minutes. Place drained liquid in a saute pan large enough to hold oysters in a single layer. Bring court bouillon to a gentle simmer and poach oysters until edges begin to curl slightly. Drain and reserve oysters.

Assembly: Saute spinach in garlic butter and season. Place an oyster in each of the puff pastry shells and top with the spinach.

Bake in oven for three minutes at 425 degrees. Serve on a warmed plate containing a light coating of the saffron sauce and drizzle the beurre blanc and beurre rouge over each oyster. Top each piece with a sprig of dill and sprinkle entire plate with chopped parsley.

Lamb Ribeye in Phyllo with Rosemary Reduction Sauce   SERVES 4

2 racks of lamb
1 onion
1 carrot
1 celery stalk
8 oz. melted butter
1 teaspoon chopped shallot
1 cup port
1 teaspoon fresh rosemary
1 lb. fresh spinach (or a 10 oz. packet frozen)
1 teaspoon chopped garlic
2 oz. unsalted butter
1 cup heavy cream
1 egg
1 box phyllo dough
1/8 cup cornmeal

Have your butcher remove the caps and completely bone the racks of lamb, reserving the caps and bones (also ask him for extra lamb bones.) Trim off excess fat and silver skin and cut each piece of meat in two. Season with salt and pepper and saute quickly in olive oil until brown on all sides. Remove and let cool.

Trim all meat from the caps and set aside. Blanch spinach and squeeze dry. Saute garlic and shallots in butter and add spinach.

Grind lamb trimmings in a food processor. Add spinach, rosemary, egg, 1 cup heavy cream and salt and pepper. Puree just until it holds together.

Place one sheet of dough onto work surface, brush with melted butter and lay another sheet over and brush with butter again. Divide lamb and spinach mixture by four. Take one portion, divide in half and place in center of dough, lay 1 piece of meat on top and cover with remaining half portion of forcemeat. Fold sheets of dough over the lamb to cover completely. Repeat procedure with remaining 3 pieces of lamb. Place on a baking sheet sprinkled with cornmeal and brush again with butter. Bake at 425 degrees for 8 to 10 minutes for medium, or until pastry is golden brown.

The following sauce is much easier made the day before:

Remove excess fat from bones and place in a large roasting pan in the oven at 350 degrees for 30 minutes. Add chopped onion, celery and carrots and roast for 15 minutes more. Drain off excess fat and remove bones and vegetables to a stockpot. Add one quart (more if necessary) of cold water (to just cover bones) and bring to a boil. Lower heat and simmer for 1½ to 2 hours until liquid is reduced to one pint. Drain stock, cool and completely degrease.

Saute ½ teaspoon shallots in butter, add port, fresh rosemary and stock and reduce to one cup. Season with salt and pepper.

To serve: Pour a little sauce on each dinner place and place lamb on top. Garnish with sprigs of fresh rosemary.

Triple-Chocolate Silk SERVES 8

vegetable oil
1 tablespoon unflavored gelatin
¼ cup cold water
5 large egg yolks at room temperature
¼ cup sugar
1 cup half-and-half, scalded
3 oz. white chocolate, finely ground
3 oz. milk chocolate, broken into small pieces
3 oz. semi-sweet chocolate, broken into small pieces
1¾ cups whipping cream, well chilled
Bittersweet Chocolate Sauce (recipe follows)

Brush inside of a 6-cup souffle dish lightly with oil and set aside. Soften gelatin in cold water; reserve. Beat the egg yolks and sugar with a whisk in a medium-sized mixer bowl until mixture becomes pale yellow and forms a ribbon (mixture dropped from a raised whisk falls in an even stream that stacks up on itself like a ribbon before sinking into the rest of the mixture.) Gradually whisk scalded half-and-half into yolk mixture.

Transfer yolk mixture to heavy 2-quart non-aluminum saucepan; cook, stirring constantly with a wooden spoon, over low heat, until mixture thickens and coats spoon, 10 to 12 minutes (do not boil). Remove from heat. Add reserved gelatin mixture to yolk mixture and stir until gelatin completely dissolves. Strain yolk mixture into 1-quart measuring container. Transfer ⅓ of mixture to each of 3 small mixing bowls. Working quickly, immediately whisk white chocolate into first bowl, milk chocolate into second bowl, and semi-sweet chocolate into the third bowl. Return to white chocolate mixture; whisk again to be sure white chocolate is completely melted and thoroughly blended. Cover bowl with lightly buttered plastic wrap (with plastic touching custard); refrigerate. Whisk, cover, and refrigerate milk chocolate mixture and semi-sweet chocolate mixture following same procedure.

Whip one cup of the cream in a chilled, small mixer bowl until stiff peaks form. Remove white chocolate mixture from refrigerator. (As each of the 3 chocolate mixtures is removed from refrigerator, it should be thick, but still viscous, similar to the consistency of unbeaten egg whites. If it is too thick, set bowl over a small amount of simmering water and stir only until of proper consistency.) Fold half of the beaten cream into white chocolate mixture; refrigerate remaining beaten cream.

Pour white chocolate mixture into reserved souffle dish; smooth top and tap dish lightly on counter to settle mixture and eliminate air bubbles. Cover dish with plastic wrap and freeze for no longer than 10 to 15 minutes. Fold remaining beaten cream into milk chocolate mixture; pour into souffle dish over set white chocolate layer. Smooth top with the back of a spoon and press gently to eliminate air bubbles. Cover with plastic wrap and freeze until milk chocolate layer is set, no longer than 10 to 15 minutes. Meanwhile, whip remaining ¾ cup cream in a chilled mixer bowl until stiff peaks form. Fold beaten cream into semi-sweet chocolate mixture; pour into souffle dish over set milk chocolate layer. Smooth top with back of a spoon and press gently to eliminate air bubbles. Cover with plastic wrap and refrigerate until Silk is completely firm, at least 4 hours, or overnight (do not freeze).

Prepare Bittersweet Chocolate Sauce (recipe follows).

Just before serving, rub bottom and sides of souffle dish with a hot damp towel until Silk loosens. Invert souffle dish onto lightly oiled plate and remove souffle dish. Refrigerate until Silk is firm again, about 5 minutes.

To serve, cut Silk into 8 wedges. Pour about ¼ cup Bittersweet Chocolate Sauce onto a large plate; tilt plate as needed to coat with sauce. Place a wedge of Silk in center of each plate on sauce and serve immediately.

Bittersweet Chocolate Sauce:

1 cup cold water
½ cup sugar
6 oz. bittersweet chocolate, broken into small pieces
2 oz. unsweetened chocolate, broken into small pieces
¼ cup lightly salted butter, cut into 4 pieces
1 tablespoon Cognac or brandy

Combine water and sugar in a one-quart non-aluminum saucepan; heat over low heat to simmering. Cover mixture and simmer for 5 minutes. Uncover, remove from heat and cool to lukewarm.

Melt bittersweet and unsweetened chocolates with butter according to directions. Gradually stir lukewarm sugar syrup into chocolate mixture; stir in Cognac. Keep sauce at room temperature until serving time, up to 4 hours. (Do not refrigerate, chocolate will harden.)

THE ARK

The Ark Restaurant is located in a prominent building right in the center of Newport, at the junction of Thames Street, Memorial Boulevard and America's Cup Avenue. The Ark is British-owned and operated by William Smith and Tim & Cathy Herring. Visiting Newport in 1980 for the America's Cup, they fell in love with the town and started to search for a suitable home for the restaurant they wanted to open in conjunction with their very successful restaurants in London. The place they found certainly seems to have been a challenge to take on, but they jumped at the chance of having the opportunity to restore a historic building and now have a guest house, restaurant and bar all in the same location.

The building was constructed in 1898 and is listed in the National Register of Historic Buildings. The upper floors were formerly operated as an inn by a Mrs. Mary Gallager, who became known as Ma Gallager to her guests. The Ark added a bit of new history to its historic past when Britain's Prince Andrew visited the restaurant for the official dinner given in his honor before the British Ball during the America's Cup Trials in 1983.

On the ground floor of the Ark is an English-style pub, authentically decorated and very much in keeping with the style and date of the building, while upstairs is a beautifully designed dining room reminiscent of an Italian garden. The creation of London designer Julie Hodges, this romantic confection in apricot, grey and pale green features handpainted stencilled wall coverings, marbelized woodwork, and painted cloud effects, set off by potted trees, Oriental carpets and exquisite drapes at the many windows. The tables are attractively set with crisp linens, fresh flowers and candles and have been arranged carefully to allow for plenty of space between parties of diners — something that seems to be a rare commodity these days.

The food served at The Ark is "progressive American cuisine with continental and international influences", say the owners, and is prepared with fresh New England produce of an exceptionally high quality. The Chef changes the menu frequently, but such dishes as halibut in a hazelnut crust with banana and chutney sauce, blackened catfish, (see following recipes for both), roasted breast of duckling with a fig and pecan sauce, ravioli of spinach and chicken, and "Steak of the Ark" (with green peppercorns, mustard, shallots and a brandy cream sauce) are often on the menu and give one an idea of the kind of food served here. The Chef's favorite recipes follow, along with his comments for each one. Desserts might include an incredibly rich chocolate terrine, Julie's famous creme brulee (see following recipe), raspberry-hazelnut sorbet, and an English trifle which is pretty close to being English. The food is beautifully presented and impeccably served. The Ark has an unpretentious and moderately-priced wine list which includes the Sakonnet America's Cup white, and the house wine is a French Burgundy, Mommesin.

During the summer months, the Ark also serves an international breakfast from 8 to 11 a.m., while lunch is served year 'round. Whether you visit the pub for lunch, have breakfast on the sidewalk terrace, or enjoy dinner in the beautiful surroundings of the dining room, you're sure to be well looked after and well fed.

THE ARK
348 Thames Street, Newport • (401) 849-3808

OPEN: all year
BREAKFAST: 8–11 am (in season only)
LUNCH: 11 am–6 pm
DINNER: 6–10 pm
SUNDAY BRUNCH: 11 am–3 pm
SEPARATE BAR: The Pub, 11:30 am–1 am
SEATS: 60–80
CHILDREN'S PORTIONS: smaller portions are served for
    lunch and dinner
RESERVATIONS: advised — call 847-3808

Grilled Shrimp

Something instead of the standard shrimp cocktail needed to be offered to the public. This is basically with a Japanese influence.

16 large shrimp, peeled & deveined
4 oz. fresh ginger, peeled & pureed
8 oz. soy sauce
2 tbs. honey
8 oz. water

Combine all ingredients and let sit overnight.

3 ea. star anise
4 oz. rice wine vinegar
3 oz. soy souce
2 oz. heavy cream
1 tsp. fresh pureed ginger
¾ lb. butter, cut into small pieces

In a heavy gauge saucepan combine the first 3 ingredients and the ginger and reduce to one-third its volume. Add heavy cream and reduce to ½ volume. Over a medium heat whisk in butter piece by piece, whipping it quickly. When fully emulsified remove from heat and cover.

    Grill shrimp over med/high heat turning often so they do not dry out, and baste with marinade. Pour a little sauce on a plate and place shrimp on sauce. Sprinkle with toasted sesame seeds and serve immediately.

Optional Garnish

Fashion a nest or basket out of fresh angel-hair pasta. Saute the nest in hot oil to produce a center piece for the shrimp to be arranged on. Garnish with a thin julienne of poached leek, carrot and beet.

Cold Canapés of Smoked Scallops
with a Ginger and Papaya Sauce   SERVES 4

I thought of this dish while doing a papaya and ginger sauce for grilled swordfish. I used to buy smoked scallops and just pop them in my mouth. I tried this recipe with the papaya and discovered a blend of tastes I thought were wonderful.

1 lb. smoked scallops
2 tablespoons ground fresh ginger
1 papaya, skinned and de-seeded
3 oz. lime juice, freshly squeezed
3 oz. white Bordeaux
4 oz. butter, cut into small cubes

Reserve 16 smoked scallops.

Stew the papaya with the ginger, lime juice and white wine until soft. Puree in food processer. Add remaining smoked scallops and puree again. Add butter cuts while spinning. Remove from processor and chill for 1 hour.

Toast thin slices of French bread and place papaya mix on top of each one. Garnish with the reserved whole smoked scallops and a sprig of arugula or mache.

Blackened Catfish with
Garlic Flavored Mayonnaise   SERVES 4

Cajun cooking has been the rage for the past few years. But I don't think that the real Cajun spices are too palatable. So cutting the mix with corn meal does two things: it cuts down the amount of "spice", as well as giving the fish more of a crust to keep it moist and flavorful.

Sauce:

4 tsp. sweetened garlic*, pureed
1 baking potato, peeled and cooked, then chilled
16 oz. extra virgin olive oil
5 egg yolks
1 tbs. salt
1 tsp. white pepper
juice of 1 lemon

   *cloves of garlic that have been poached in cold water five times.

In a food processor puree potato and sweet garlic. Add egg yolks and puree to a fine consistency. Slowly add the olive oil. When finished add lemon juice, salt and pepper.

Cajun Blackening Mix:

2 tbs. gumbofile
2 tbs. cayenne pepper
2 tbs. white pepper
2 tbs. black pepper   Mix thoroughly
2 tbs. paprika
2 tbs. garlic powder
2 tbs. onion powder
14 tbs. corn meal

Catfish:

3 oz. butter
4 6-oz. boneless catfish per person
Cajun blackening mix
14" cast iron skillet

Dredge catfish in Cajun mix. Heat skillet to maximum temperature. Add butter and sear filets for 2½—3 minutes on both sides.

Spread sauce on four plates and serve well drained fish on top. Accompany fish with grilled vegetables such as a ½" slice of Bermuda onion with thyme, jalapenos, ½" slice of ripe tomato with chopped basil, or grilled corn wedges.

Ravioli of Chicken and Spinach with a Sweet Garlic Cream   SERVES 4

The sweetness of the garlic is achieved merely by taking the oil and acidity out of the garlic. In the restaurant we use elephant garlic which is milder than normal garlic and easier to work with. Sweet garlic gives you the flavor but very little of the "scampi breath" associated with garlic.

Stuffing:

10 oz. fresh spinach, steamed, chilled and drained
12 oz. chicken breast boned, skinned and poached
3 whole eggs
2 tbs. sweet garlic, crushed
1 tsp. salt
½ tsp. white pepper

Put chicken in the food processor and puree fine. Add eggs, garlic, salt, pepper and puree until fine. Spoon mixture into a mixing bowl, fold in the coarsely chopped spinach and chill.

Cut fresh sheet pasta with a 4—4½" round cookie or pastry cutter. Keep reserved and moist with a wet cloth. Using an egg wash and a pastry brush, brush one side of each circle, doing only 12 at a time. Place a tablespoon of mixture on one side of round and with your fingers crimp them in half so they resemble a moon in the quarter phase. When finished place on a flat pan large enough to fit in the freezer.

Garlic Cream:

16 oz. heavy cream	**2 oz. sweet (unsalted) butter**
2 oz. sweet garlic, pureed	**1 tsp. salt**
1 oz. arrowroot	**½ tsp. white ground pepper**

Bring heavy cream and sweet garlic to the scalding point, being careful not to boil. Slowly add arrowroot mixture and whisk briskly. Season with salt and pepper. Remove from heat and whip in the butter.

Poach ravioli for approximately 7—10 minutes in salted water and serve with sauce on top.

Serving option:

Clean one more 10 oz. bag of spinach and saute the raw spinach in 2 oz. of butter seasoned with salt and pepper and make a ring of wilted spinach around the plate. Place ravioli on the inside of the ring with sauce and garnish with fresh snips of chives and pink peppercorn.

Halibut in a Hazelnut Crust
with Banana and Chutney Sauce   SERVES 4

Halibut:

4 6-oz. boned and skinned halibut filets, approx. ½" thick
1 lb. whole hazelnuts, ground fine and sifted
2 eggs and 4 oz. water combined
flour to pat on fish
4 oz. clarified butter

Pre-heat oven to 425 degrees.

Take 3 plates and place the flour in the first, the egg and water in the second and the ground hazelnuts in the third. Bread the filets first in the flour, then in the egg mix, and then in the hazelnuts.

Heat the butter gently in a oven proof skillet. When hot, place the filets in the skillet. Cook for 2 minutes. Turn, and place the skillet in the oven for approximately 10 — 12 minutes. Remove fish from pan and served immediately with the banana and chutney sauce.

Sauce:

bones from halibut, approx. 1 lb.
16 oz. white wine
4 tbs. chopped shallots
16 oz. heavy cream
8 oz. chutney
2 bananas

Place fish bones, shallots and white wine in a heavy saucepan and reduce to half its volume. Add heavy cream to this and reduce again to half its volume. Strain sauce into another saucepan and add the chutney and cut up bananas. Bring sauce to a boil and remove from heat. Puree sauce in either a food processor or a blender. Cover and keep warm until ready to serve.

Garnish with chive flowers and a julienne of pickled ginger, or a caramelized wedge of banana, or a fanned poached apple could be used.

Julie's Crème Brûlée   SERVES 4

This is a famous dish from the Ark's sister restaurant, Julie's, in London. It was a feat trying to duplicate it with American rather than English cream.

6 egg yolks
1 cup heavy cream
1 tsp. vanilla
3 oz. raw sugar

Using a saucepan as a bottom of a double boiler and snug fitting aluminum bowl as a top, bring water to a boil. Add all ingredients to boiler and briskly beat until mixture thickens. Remove from heat and continue to whip so the custard cools slightly. Pour custard into oven proof ramekins or custard dishes (approximately 4 oz. each) hopefully as wide as tall. Place in freezer for 6 hours to set.

To serve:

Pre-heat broiler. Remove brulees from freezer and place about a ¼'' depth of raw sugar on top of each and place under the broiler until the sugar caramelize and starts to burn around the edges. Remove and place on individual serving plates. Allow brulees to stand 1 minute to cool and let sugar harden like a crisp toffee. The brulee will have a frozen ice cream-like bottom and a cool liquid top, then the hard crisp toffee on top.

THE RHUMBLINE

The Rhumbline is the only restaurant/tavern located in the historic Point section of Newport. Here, Colonial clapboard buildings painted muted shades of green and blue, red and brown, line quiet gaslit streets and transport one back to the time of the old 18th century port. The Rhumbline is an integral part of its surroundings, and it is with an element of pleasant surprise that, on entering the restaurant, visitors are welcomed by a tastefully modernized interior with handsome natural pine partitions and fitments. Bare floorboards, hanging plants, terracotta-colored table coverings and crisp white napkins create an unpretentious and comfortable atmosphere which immediately makes guests feel at home.

The Rhumbline has been owned since 1980 by Stephen Giunta, a lobster fisherman who transformed this local gin mill into a charming setting for contemporary dining. The Chef describes the food as "nutritious and delicious—from the basic to gourmet" . . . fresh ingredients predominate, and homemade stocks are used as a base for soups and sauces. The menu is varied and is augmented by innovative daily blackboard items. Specialties include Weinerschnitzel, stuffed seafood, prime rib, curried mussel soup (see recipe), lobster (in season), and a simple but delicious dessert, chocolate bread pudding topped with French ice cream. The wine list contains some fine selections, and—good news for solo wine drinkers—quality imported wines are available by the glass.

The Rhumbline succeeds admirably in its goal to create a genuinely friendly meeting place where visitors can enjoy excellent food and drink in convivial surroundings which manage to retain the unmistakable flavor of the Point neighborhood. Lunch and dinner are served year 'round, with brunch on Sundays, and there's live jazz on Friday and Saturday evenings.

THE RHUMBLINE

62 Bridge Street, Newport • (401) 849-6950

Open all year, seven days a week, except
  Thanksgiving and Christmas
OPEN: 11:30 a.m. to 1:00 a.m.
LUNCH: 11:30 a.m. to 3:00 p.m.
DINNER: 5:00 to 10:00 p.m., weekends until 11:00 p.m.
SUNDAY BRUNCH: 11:30 a.m. to 4:00 p.m.
SEATS: 65
CHILDREN'S PORTIONS: not served
CREDIT CARDS: MC & VISA
PARKING: private lot and off-street parking
RESERVATIONS: off season only

Curried Mussel Soup

SERVES 4

2 qts. fresh mussels
½ cup chopped shallots
1 tablespoon minced garlic
1 tablespoon chopped parsley
2 cups white wine
1½ tablespoons curry powder
1 tablespoon brown sugar
2 tablespoons butter
2 tablespoons flour

Place mussels, shallots, garlic, parsley and wine into a large saucepan. Steam mussels to open. Strain and reserve broth. Pull mussels from shells and reserve the meat. Return broth to saucepan and add 3 cups water. Bring to simmer. Add curry powder and brown sugar.

Make a roux with the butter and flour and add to the seasoned broth to thicken slightly. Add salt and pepper to taste, add mussels and let soup simmer 20 minutes, stirring occasionally to avoid burning bottom of pot.

Chicken Livers Moutarde

SERVES 4

2 lbs. chicken livers
Flour
2 tablespoons chopped shallots
1 teaspoon minced garlic
¼ cup Marsala wine
3 tablespoons Dijon mustard
½ cup light cream
Salt and pepper to taste
Chopped parsley to garnish
4 slices bread, toasted, crusts cut off,
 and cut into 4 triangles each

Soak livers in milk for thirty minutes to remove any excess blood. Drain, rinse and pat dry. Coat the bottom of a large skillet or saute pan with olive oil and allow to heat until oil just starts to smoke. Dust livers with flour and carefully place into the hot oil. Brown livers evenly until thoroughly cooked. Remove from pan. Using more oil if needed, saute the shallots and garlic until translucent. Add the wine, mustard and cream. Stir to blend and then simmer sauce until slightly thickened. Season to taste with salt and pepper. Pour sauce into warm serving plates and arrange toast points (4 on each plate) in desired fashion. Top each with 1-2 chicken livers. Serve immediately.

Veal & Shrimp a la Creme

SERVES 4

4 6 oz. veal leg cutlets
2 tablespoons chopped shallots
8 jumbo shrimp, peeled, deveined & butterflied
6 large mushrooms, sliced thin
¼ pound Proscuitto ham, finely julienned
½ cup white wine
½ cup heavy cream
2 tablespoons fresh sage
 (or 1 tablespoon dried sage)
Salt & pepper to taste

Coat bottom of large saute pan with olive oil and allow to heat. Dust the veal slices with flour and brown quickly. Remove from pan. Saute shallots, shrimp and mushrooms together until shrimp are just under-done. Add wine and bring to simmer. Add cream, sage, salt and pepper. Return veal to sauce and simmer to reduce until slightly thickened. Add ham. Serve with rice or pasta.

Amaretto Cheese Pie

1 lb. cream cheese
5 eggs
⅓ cup sugar
1 - 2 oz. Amaretto liqueur

Topping:
¾ cup sour cream
¼ teaspoon vanilla essense
3 tablespoons sugar

Cream the cream cheese and sugar together until light and fluffy. Add eggs and blend well. Add Amaretto and blend in.

Pour into pyrex pie dish (9" or 10") and bake at 325 degrees for approximately 40 minutes or until pie rises and center is cooked. Over-baking will cause cracking. Remove from oven and allow pie to fall.

Mix the ingredients for the topping together. Spread over the top of the pie and return to oven for 5 minutes to set topping.

Rhumᵇline

Restaurant
Tavern

INN AT CASTLE HILL

The **Inn at Castle Hill** sits majestically atop a bluff overlooking the clear blue water of the East Passage where the Atlantic Ocean funnels into Narraganett Bay. This mansion, set in thirty-two acres of grounds, was built in 1884 as a summer home for the renowned scientist and explorer Alexander Agassiz.

The rambling building has been converted into an elegant country inn and every effort made to maintain the original home-like atmosphere. Agassiz' personal collection of Japanese and Chinese art and antiques have been added to over the years and lend an exotic flavor to the Victorian interior. Graciously-appointed reception rooms are lavishly panelled with hand-carved mahogany, oak and pine, and Oriental rugs cover polished floorboards. The dining rooms, decorated with antiques and old sporting prints, all have magnificent views of the water and for summer dining, a spacious garden room overlooking rolling lawns and the bay beyond has been added to the original building. A welcoming sitting room with open fireplace and a lively lounge/bar provide comfortable gathering places where house guests and visitors can meet for cocktails and listen to live piano music or jazz.

For many of its guests, the ultimate charm of Castle Hill lies in the natural beauty of the hilly peninsula over which the Inn presides. However, the innkeeper is aware that guests may not wish to be sustained by nature alone and has thoughtfully provided elegant dining rooms and a menu featuring continental cuisine. The chef believes in serving only the freshest ingredients and offers a mainly classical menu, featuring traditional favorites such as *escargot bourguignonne*, pate, rack of lamb, and New England lobster, as well as some more unusual dishes such as fresh moulard duck liver sauteed and served with sauce Normande, garnished with baked, sliced apples; sweetbread with fresh duck liver and truffle sauce; and poached halibut filled with lobster mousse and served with caviar-butter sauce. An extensive selection of fine French and Californian wines complements the menu. For dessert try the *vacherin romanoff*, meringue shells filled with fresh strawberries marinated in Grand Marnier and topped with whipped cream, or the white chocolate mousse (recipes follow for both desserts). Sunday brunch accompanied by live music, usually jazz, is a special attraction, served from noon until 4 p.m. In summer, there's also afternoon New Orleans jazz on the expansive lawn that slopes towards the water.

To visit the Inn at Castle Hill is to step back in time to the era of the Newport "cottage", when the pace of life was slower and certain standards were higher. These elusive elements are captured perfectly at this romantic and hospitable country inn, adding a new dimension to the enjoyment of dining out.

THE INN AT CASTLE HILL
Ocean Drive, Newport • (401) 849-3800

OPEN: seven days a week, all year
  (rooms only year 'round)
CLOSED: for dinner on Sunday night and lunch on Monday
CONTINENTAL BREAKFAST: 8:00 to 10:00 a.m. (house guests only)
LUNCH: 12 noon to 2:30 p.m., Memorial Day Weekend to Oct. 31st
DINNER: From 6:00 p.m. every night except Sunday
SUNDAY BRUNCH: 12 noon to 4:00 p.m., April to January 1
SEATS: 140
CHILDREN'S PORTIONS: not available
CREDIT CARDS: AMEX, MC, VISA
PARKING: ample

Hot Potato & Leek Soup
Vichyssoise

3 bunches of leeks
4 lb. potatoes
1 oz. bay leaves
1½ lb. onions
1 qt. milk
Salt and white pepper

Peel the potatoes and onions. Cut off green part of leeks and discard. Chop potatoes, onions and white part of leeks into large pieces and place in a large saucepan. Cover with double the volume of water. Bring to a boil. Add bay leaves and simmer for 4 to 5 hours. Work soup through a food mill or puree in a blender or food processor. Add milk, salt and pepper to taste. Heavy cream may be added for a creamier flavor. Serve hot.

Poached Oysters with Caviar   SERVES 4

2 lb. shucked oysters
1 glass of dry sherry
2 oz. red salmon caviar
2 oz. roux
1 cup heavy cream
Small bag of bouquet garni
Fleurons

Mix together oysters and their juice with the sherry and bouquet garni. Poach for three minutes. Remove oysters and set aside in a warm place. Add roux to the liquid and cook it for five minutes, stirring well. Add the heavy cream and heat through. Add the oysters and serve immediately. Garnish with caviar and fleurons.

Filet De Canard Aux Trois Poivres
Duck Breast with Three-Peppercorn Sauce

Per Person:

1 duck breast, skinned
1 tablespoon crushed pink, green and black
peppercorns
1 tablespoon duck fat
3 tablespoons heavy cream
1 tablespoon brandy
1 pinch tarragon reduction
½ lb. cooked wild rice
Pinch of salt

Flatten duck breast with a mallet. Heat pan and add duck fat. Saute duck breast for about one minute on each side. Remove from pan.

Deglaze pan with brandy. Add peppercorns, cream and tarragon reduction. Add salt to taste and reduce sauce until thickened. In the meantime, slice duck into thin strips. Arrange wild rice on a platter and pour the sauce around it. Arrange sliced duck on top. The duck should be cooked rare to medium-rare.

Eileen's Au Gratin   SERVES 6—8

5 lb. potatoes
½ lb. butter
1 cup grated parmesan cheese
Salt and pepper
1 quart Half & Half

Boil the unpeeled potatoes until half cooked. Cool completely in the refrigerator. Peel the potatoes, grate them and place in a hotel pan. Add salt and pepper.

Fill the pan with potatoes and Half & Half until it almost covers the potatoes. Sprinkle Parmesan cheese on top of the potatoes. Dot the top with butter cut into small pieces. Bake in oven for 45 minutes at 350 degrees until the top is brown and crusty.

Vacherin Romanoff

10 ready-made small meringue shells
1 pint fresh strawberries
1 cup orange juice
Zest of one orange
2 oz. Grand Marnier
Whipped cream

Slice the strawberries and marinate them in orange juice, zest and Grand Marnier. Arrange on meringue shells just before serving. Sprinkle top with a little Grand Marnier and decorate with whipped cream.

White Chocolate Mousse "Sabra"

½ lb. white chocolate
2 oz. unflavored gelatin
3 cups heavy cream
2 oz. Sabra Liqueur
2 cups milk
Zest from one orange

Melt the chocolate with milk until it is smooth. Add Sabra Liqueur and the unflavored gelatin (previously soaked in cold milk). Place in a stainless steel bowl and chill on ice.

In the meantime, whip the heavy cream until soft peaks form. Carefully fold the cream into the chocolate mixture. Divide the chocolate mousse into serving dishes and chill at least three hours before serving. Decorate with orange zest soaked in Sabra Liqueur. Bon appetit!

BRICK ALLEY PUB & RESTAURANT

Right across Thames Street from the Brick Market Place is the **Brick Alley Pub & Restaurant,** a lively watering hole that offers a wide selection of food and drink ranging from appetizers, burgers, tacos, sandwiches, omelets, desserts and "potent potables" to a changing daily menu of lunch and dinner entrees.

A smoothly run and professionally managed operation, the Brick Alley Pub & Restaurant was opened in 1980 by Ralph and Pat Plumb following training at the School of Hotel and Restaurant Management at Cornell University and then a career in managing restaurants across the country, from Los Angeles to Pittsburgh, and up and down the East and West Coasts. While doing all this traveling, they had the opportunity to sample many different restaurants, gathering ideas for what could become the Brick Alley Pub & Restaurant's diverse menu and eclectic decor.

The corner location Ralph and Pat chose for their restaurant, a dignified building which formerly housed the Newport Daily News, has been snappily refurbished with yellow and white striped awnings, cafe-style curtains in the tall street-front windows and hanging potted plants. Artifacts and nostalgia collected from all over North America by the owners decorate the interior. Blackboards display daily specials, and samplings might include such varied dishes as sole Vanderbilt, steak au poivre (see following recipe for both), Cajun-style scallops, fresh garlic parsley linguine with jumbo shrimp and julienne vegetables, sweet & sour chicken and spinach fettuccine alfredo, as well as some wonderful-sounding desserts, including Milky Way cake.

A special feature is the soup and salad buffet, serving freshly-prepared soup of the day and a selection of chilled, crisp greens and vegetables. Another specialty is the Irish Coffee, three-times the winner of the Jameson Irish Whiskey Cup, awarded to the best Irish Coffee served on Aquidneck Island.

Sunday Brunch at the Brick Alley Pub & Restaurant is an excellent deal. Entrees range from steak & eggs to eggs Sardou and include a special fruit and salad buffet. Also available is the most exotic collection of cocktails, daiquiris and coladas one could wish to find anywhere; how about trying a Slow Train to Mazatlan—a frosty concoction of fresh strawberries, bananas, peach brandy, light and dark rum, served in a pint Mason jar. And for the designated driver of the evening there are "mocktails", non-alcoholic fruit smoothies, and Kaliber (non-alcoholic) beer.

Ralph and Pat Plumb's goal is to provide their guests with the finest quality in food, service and atmosphere, after all "there is hardly anything in the world that some person cannot make a little worse and sell a little cheaper; and people who consider price alone are this person's lawful prey." But Ralph and Pat haven't forgotten that what people also want is to have fun, and at the Brick Alley Pub & Restaurant you will eat well, drink well and have a good time, too.

BRICK ALLEY PUB & RESTAURANT
140 Thames Street, Newport • (401) 849-8291/849-6334

OPEN: All year
LUNCH: 11:00 a.m. — 5:00 p.m.
DINNER: 5:00 p.m. — 11:00
SUNDAY BRUNCH: 11:00 a.m. — 3:00 p.m.
SEATS: 72 off season; 125 summer
CHILDREN'S PORTIONS: Always available
CREDIT CARDS: MC, VISA, CB, DINERS, AMEX;
        R.I. Personal checks accepted
RESERVATIONS: Only two reservations taken per half hour;
        other tables left open for walk-in business

Chilled Strawberry Soup

Make 1½ quarts

1½ cups water
1 cup Beaujolais wine
½ cup sugar
2 tbs. fresh lemon juice
1 cinnamon stick
1 qt. strawberries, hulled and pureed
½ cup whipping cream
¼ cup sour cream

Combine water, wine, sugar, lemon juice and cinnamon stick in a 4-quart saucepan and boil uncovered 10 minutes, stirring occasionally. Add strawberry puree and boil, stirring frequently for 10 minutes more. Discard cinnamon stick and let soup cool.

Whip cream. Combine with sour cream and fold into strawberry mixture. Serve chilled.

Escargot-Stuffed Mushrooms

SERVES 4

24 washed medium sized button mushrooms
1 cup seasoned buttered breadcrumbs
1 tbs. chopped scallions
6 slices raw bacon
1 tbs. chopped parsley
24 helix snails
2 oz. cognac
1 tsp. minced garlic
½ lb. garlic butter
1 dash nutmeg

Marinate escargots overnight in a mixture of minced garlic, cognac, scallions, nutmeg and chopped parsley.

Blanch mushrooms in boiling water until half cooked. Cool and remove stems from mushroom caps. Put a scant teaspoon of garlic butter in each mushroom cap. Place one escargot in each mushroom cap. Top each mushroom with seasoned buttered breadcrumbs and ¼ strip of bacon. Bake in pre-heated 400⁰ oven until bacon is crisp.

Sole Vanderbilt

Per person

2 fillets of sole
¼ cup fresh sea scallops
¼ cup snow crab
¼ cup shredded cheddar or Monterey Jack cheese
¼ cup sliced mushrooms
½ oz. white wine
1 tbs. garlic butter
1 tbs. buttered bread crumbs
½ cup hollandaise sauce *(see following recipe)*

Preheat oven to 450⁰. Spread garlic butter in an individual casserole. Place one sole fillet on bottom of casserole and place a layer of scallops on top of the filet; then layer on the crabmeat, mushrooms and cheese. Add a splash of white wine. Top with second fillet of sole and sprinkle with buttered bread crumbs. Bake until fish flakes, 10—15 minutes. Top with warm hollandaise sauce and sprinkle with paprika before serving.

Hollandaise Sauce

Makes approximately 1½ cups

¼ cup water (or white wine)
1½ tbs. fresh lemon juice
¼ tsp. salt
pinch white pepper
3 egg yolks
1 cup (2 sticks) unsalted butter

Mix water, lemon juice, salt and pepper in a small saucepan. Bring to boil, reduce heat and simmer until liquid is reduced to two tablespoons. Set pan in larger pan of cold water to cool.

Beat egg yolks in a non-aluminum saucepan until thick and creamy. Slowly beat in lemon reduction. Whisk over low heat until thickened. Do not allow eggs to become too thick or dry. Remove from heat and begin slowly drizzling warm, not hot, melted butter into the yolks, beating constantly until all the butter has been incorporated and the sauce is just pourable.

Seafood Quiche

½ cup mayonnaise
2 tbs. flour
3 eggs
½ cup milk
½ lb. snow crab meat
½ lb. scallops
½ lb. Swiss cheese, shredded
½ cup scallions, diced
½ cup mushrooms, sliced
½ oz. sherry
1 pie shell

Pre-bake shell for 5 minutes at 375⁰.
    Whip until frothy: mayonnaise, flour, eggs, milk and sherry. Immediately stir in: Swiss cheese, crabmeat, scallops, mushrooms and scallions.
    Pour all ingredients into pre-baked pie shell. Bake at 325⁰ for 30 minutes, or until slightly golden brown on top. Remove from oven. Let stand for one hour before serving.

New York Sirloin Au Poivre

1 12 oz. boneless prime New York sirloin steak
1 tbs. coarsely cracked black pepper
¼ cup cognac
¼ cup heavy cream
1 tsp. Dijon mustard

Trim excess fat from steak and pound it until thin, to about ½ of original thickness. Render excess fat trimmings in a heavy skillet over high heat. Press cracked pepper into both sides of meat. Remove unrendered fat from skillet, add steaks and sear one minute on each side. Reduce heat and continue cooking until desired doneness is *almost* achieved. Transfer steak to heated plate and keep warm while preparing sauce.
    Pour off excess fat in skillet. Deglaze pan by adding cognac. Blend in cream and mustard and cook over high heat until sauce thickens. Pour sauce over steak and serve immediately.

Chocolate Mousse

SERVES 6

4 oz. semi-sweet chocolate, broken up into small pieces
1 pint whipping cream
3 large egg yolks
4 oz. sugar

Place chocolate in a double boiler and melt slowly over a low flame. Be very careful not to burn chocolate.

Whip heavy cream in a large stainless steel bowl until firm. Hold under refrigeration until needed.

Combine yolks and sugar in a stainless steel bowl and whip thoroughly. Temper the eggs by adding a small amount of chocolate to the egg and sugar mixture and whip well. Add remaining melted chocolate and whip until smooth.

Fold chocolate mixture into whipped cream by folding in gently with a rubber spatula. Be sure to mix all ingredients thoroughly.

Fill 7 ounce stemmed glasses with mousse to ½ inch from the top.

Refrigerate for four hours to allow the mousse to set.

Remove from refrigerator and top with whipped cream and chocolate shavings. We recommend Ghiardelli chocolate from San Francisco.

Hot Apple Pie Cocktail

SERVES 4

1 qt. apple cider
4 cloves
6 oz. Tuaca

½ pint whipping cream
4 cinnamon sticks

Bring apple cider and cloves to a boil in a medium saucepan. Pour Tuaca into four Irish coffee mugs (or stemmed glasses). Strain hot cider into glasses to within ½ inch of the rim. Top with whipped cream and a cinnamon stick.

"Brick Alley Pub & Restaurant Irish Coffee"
Winner 1983 — Jamesons Irish Whiskey Cup

Dip the rim of an Irish Coffee cup ¼" deep in a shallow saucer of Grand Marnier Liqueur. Dip the rim into a saucer of granulated sugar. Caramelize the sugar on the rim of the glass over an open flame. Add ½ tsp. of superfine sugar. Add 1½ oz. Jamesons Irish Whiskey. Fill to ½" of top with freshly brewed coffee. Top with whipped cream. Drizzle Bailey's Irish Cream liqueur over the whipped cream. Sprinkle shaved Ghiardelli chocolate over the whipped cream. Serve with a rolled wafer cookie and a sip stick.

LE BISTRO

John and Mary Philcox opened the original **Le Bistro** amongst modest surroundings at 250 Thames Street in 1974. In six years their popular restaurant had outgrown its premises and so they moved to a new and very different location in Bowen's Wharf in 1980.

The tall wooden building which is now home to Le Bistro is modern and interestingly designed inside. Climbing the winding stairs on entering, the impression one gets is of different shaped spaces divided by wooden beams and open-tread stairs, reaching on up to the bar at the top, a relaxing and informal area affording a superb view of the harbor and activity of the wharf below.

Le Bistro is divided into two distinct sections—upstairs is the bar where lunch and daily specials are served continuously all day from 11:30 a.m. to 11:00 p.m., while downstairs on the main floor lunch and dinner are served daily during specific hours.

The son of a diplomat, John lived in Paris from the age of 10 until he was 18 and became such a fan of French cuisine that he developed a passion for cooking. During a stint in the Navy, he studied the theory of the great French chefs and resolved to one day open his own restaurant. The result is an uncompromisingly authentic "bistro", from the Kir aperitif to the crusty French bread served with sweet butter. "Although I describe the menu as 'modern French'", explains John, tall, bearded and amiable, "I really don't think of it as French in an ethnic sense. My gastronomic background is French and many of my dishes are traditional French 'standards'. My main intent is to find interesting and unusual ways to use the freshest and best local products. The word 'modern' means the 'nouvelle cuisine' style and techniques. Sauces are made with a light touch and are meant to enhance and emphasize the natural goodness of the products used."

The menu changes every month or so and consists of maybe a dozen main dishes, many of which could easily outdo the creations of stylish establishments on the banks of the Seine. Recent appetizers on the menu included squash blossoms with goat cheese, scallops with beets in pastry (see following recipe), peasant pate, and palm and avocado with Vermont chevre; main courses included grilled duck with figs, salmon in champagne sabayon, bouillabaisse with rouille, and veal kidneys in a mustard and brandy sauce. The scrumptious desserts are made on the premises and include Le Bistro's renowned chocolate walnut cake made with brandy butter filling and apricot glaze (see recipe).

An excellent selection of French wines dominate the wine list, a dozen of which are available by the glass. Wines from the Sakonnet Vineyard in Little Compton, Rhode Island, also feature on the wine list. The house wine, "Private Reserve", is specially blended for Le Bistro by Sakonnet Vineyards.

The skill and devotion John lavishes on his widely-acclaimed versions of classic French cuisine have guaranteed his success as a restaurateur and established Le Bistro's reputation as a shining star amongst Newport's many fine restaurants.

LE BISTRO
Bowen's Wharf, Newport • (401) 849-7778

OPEN: 11:30 a.m. to 11:00 p.m, seven days a week
CLOSED: Thanksgiving and Christmas
LUNCH: 11:30 a.m. to 11:00 p.m.
DINNER: 6:00 to 10:00 p.m.
LATE SUPPER: served all day to 11:00 p.m.
BRUNCH: 11:30 a.m. to 2:30 p.m., Saturday & Sunday
SEATS: 85
CHILDREN'S PORTIONS: not available
SEPARATE BAR: 11:30 a.m. to 1:00 a.m.
CREDIT CARDS: AMEX, CB, DC, MC, VISA
PARKING: on Bowen's Wharf, one hour free with validation
        before 6 p.m.
RESERVATIONS: advised, call 849-7778

Terrine De Légumes
(Vegetable Terrine)

The Vegetables:
¼ lb. green beans
6 artichoke hearts
¾ lb. carrots
¾ lb. peas
grape vine leaves
salt

Trim the beans, peel the carrots, and trim the artichoke hearts. Cook the vegetables, except the peas, separately in salted water until just barely done. Do not cook the peas yet. Everything will cook again later.

The ham filling:

10 oz. ham
½ cup peanut oil
juice of one lemon
1 egg white
4 g. salt
2 g. pepper

Trim the ham carefully and cut into small dice. Put it in the food processor with the egg white, salt and pepper. Puree it and gradually add the lemon juice and oil.

The fresh tomato sauce:
1 lb. tomatoes
1 teaspoon tomato paste
salt and pepper
1½ tablespoons wine vinegar
¼ cup olive oil
tarragon, parsley

The tomatoes must be very ripe and fresh. Peel them and remove the seeds and juice. Puree the pulp in the food processor or blender. Beat in the tomato paste, then slowly beat in the vinegar and oil. Season with salt, pepper, tarragon and parsley.

Assembling the terrine:

Choose a mold about 10" x 3" x 3" and line the bottom and sides with the grape leaves. Start by putting a thin layer of the ham filling on the bottom, then a layer of carrots, then successive layers of beans, artichokes, and peas each separated by a layer of the ham filling. Cover the top with grape leaves. Cover the mold and place it in a shallow pan of water in the oven. Bake at 350 degrees for about 30 minutes. Then let it cool and refrigerate overnight. Unmold the terrine and cut into slices. Serve on chilled plates with chilled tomato sauce.

Salmon in Champagne Sabayon SERVES 4

2 lbs. salmon
2 tablespoons butter
1 tomato, peeled, seeded and chopped
1 sprig of chervil (or parsley)
¾ cup Hollandaise sauce
1 cup Champagne
¼ cup whipped cream

If possible, obtain a boneless filet of salmon. Cut into four thin slices (called scallops or escalopes). Cook the slices of salmon in a saute pan in the butter until just done. Remove and keep hot. Pour off the cooking butter. Pour in the Champagne and reduce it to half. Add the Hollandaise, tomatoes and chervil, then stir in the whipped cream. Pour the sauce around the salmon slices on a heated platter. Serve with the remaining Champagne.

Rognons de Veau
Flambés a l'Armagnac SERVES 1

Per person:
2 veal kidneys
¼ cup Armagnac
½ cup Madeira
2 tablespoons heavy cream
1 tablespoon butter
1 tablespoon Dijon mustard
fine herbes: parsley, chives, chervil, basil, tarragon
salt and pepper

Choose a pan that will just hold the kidneys comfortably. Saute them in a little butter over a moderately high flame until just barely done. They should still be quite pink and juicy on the inside. Remove the kidneys to a plate and keep in a warm place to rest a few minutes while you make the sauce.

Pour in the Armagnac and ignite. When the flames go out, add the Madeira and reduce by two thirds. Then add the cream and reduce again, boiling until the sauce has slightly thickened. Now slice the kidneys and return them to the sauce along with any juice which has dripped out of them. Add the butter, mustard and herbs. Heat gently, being careful not to overcook the kidneys. Season with salt and pepper, and serve right from the pan.

Feuillette de St. Jacques aux Betteraves Rouges

(Scallops with beets in pastry)   SERVES 4

1 lb. puff pastry
1¼ lb. scallops
4 tablespoons butter
1 fresh raw beet
1½ cups heavy cream
Salt and pepper

Use your favorite recipe for puff pastry or buy it frozen in sheets. In either case, give it a final turn and roll it out to about ¼" thick. Cut into the shape of 4 scallop shells (both parts). Brush with egg glaze (one egg beaten with one tablespoon of water) and bake for about ten minutes at 450 degrees. When the pastry shells are done, keep them warm while you cook the scallops.

Cut the raw beet into fine julienne strips, about the size of matchsticks. Heat 2 tablespoons of butter in a saute pan and cook the beets for one minute. Then add the scallops and toss them with the beets until they just begin to cook. Add the cream and cook over high heat, boiling to reduce, and cooking the scallops at the same time. In one or two minutes, the scallops should be done and the cream should be fairly thick. If the scallops are done before the cream, remove them and finish the sauce, putting the scallops back in to reheat at the end. When the cream is slightly thickened, season with salt and pepper and swirl in the remaining 2 tablespoons of butter which will complete the thickening of the sauce. Now split the pastry shells in half, pour on the scallops in sauce, and replace the top half of the shells. A garnish of fresh parsley sets off the brilliant beet-colored cream sauce.

Chocolate Walnut Cake

The Cake:

3 large eggs
1½ cups sugar
1/8 teaspoon salt
2 teaspoons vanilla extract
1½ cups flour
2 teaspoons baking powder
1½ cups heavy cream
4 oz. walnuts, pulverized in a processor

Beat the sugar and eggs together until thick and pale, then beat in the salt and vanilla. In another bowl, whip the cream until firm but soft. Now sift the flour and baking powder together and gently fold into the eggs, then fold in the whipped cream and nuts.

Turn the mixture into two buttered and floured 9 inch cake pans. Bake at 350 degrees until done, about 25 minutes. Let cool for ten minutes, then unmold onto a rack.

Brandy butter filling:

1 egg
3 tablespoons Cognac or brandy
2 tablespoons butter
½ tablespoon cornstarch
1 cup sugar
3 tablespoons butter

Beat together the egg, 2 tablespoons butter, brandy, cornstarch, and sugar. Boil for 2 minutes to cook the starch, then stir in the 3 tablespoons of butter.

Chocolate butter cream:

½ cup sugar
2½ tablespoons water
4 egg yolks
½ cup butter, soft, cut into pieces
3 oz. sweet chocolate, melted

Boil the sugar with the water until it reaches 250 degrees. Meanwhile, whip the egg yolks until they are thick. Then dribble the boiling syrup into the egg yolks, beating constantly. Continue beating until cool. Add the butter and chocolate, and beat at low speed for five more minutes.

Assembling the cake:

Spread the brandy butter over the top of one of the cakes and place the second layer on top. Then strain some apricot preserves and cook for a few seconds in a small pan. Spread this aprocit glaze around the sides of the cake, and coat the sides with crushed walnuts. Top with chocolate butter cream.

Pear Sherbet   SERVES 6

2 cups water
1 cup sugar
1 tablespoon lemon juice
½ vanilla bean, split lengthwise
6 medium-sized pears
1 egg white, beaten
pear brandy (Eau-de-Vie de Poire)

Bring the water to a boil with the sugar, lemon juice, and vanilla. Peel the pears, cut them in half and remove the cores. Poach them in the syrup until soft. Then remove the pears and puree them. Reduce the poaching syrup to one cup and add to the pureed pears. Chill thoroughly. Just before freezing, stir in the beaten egg white. Then freeze in whatever contraption you like. To serve, garnish each dish with a small slice of poached pear which you reserved for this purpose, and top with one tablespoon of pear brandy.

CANFIELD HOUSE

The Canfield House, one of Newport's most elegant restaurants, enjoyed a colorful past as a gambling casino during Newport's gilded age. Richard A. Canfield, a native of New Bedford and, incidentally, the inventor of the card game Solitaire, was a gambler of world renown. He built the most plush gambling casino in the United States in New York City and expanded to Saratoga Springs in 1894 and Newport in 1897. He ran his casino in the Canfield House until 1905, catering to a wealthy and aristocratic clientele who appreciated the lavish surroundings and sophisticated atmosphere he provided. Canfield served gourmet meals in all his casinos, a tradition carried on today by the Canfield House restaurant.

Although there's not a particularly spectacular view from the Canfield House's windows, you'll find there is plenty about the interior on which to feast the eye. Opulently decorated with dark wood raised paneling, period furniture, stained glass and a unique vaulted ceiling, the Victorian mood remains intact. Gas jets have been electrified and small dining tables have taken the place of gaming tables in the richly-paneled salon, now an elegant dining room serving distinguished American and continental cuisine.

The Canfield House has been owned since 1976 by Dianne Whitehead and her brother James Whitehead and under their guidance the business has enjoyed steady growth and continued success. The entire establishment is run in a leisurely and unhurried manner, and the service is gracious and friendly.

The basic menu consists of veal, chicken and beef dishes, with fresh native seafood obtained daily from Newport's waterfront. Five or six evening specials are also offered; the selection changes daily and might include a hearty steak and kidney pie (see following recipe). The Canfield House is well-known for its Chateaubriand, a succulent cut served with sauce bearnaise and a bouquetier of fresh vegetables. Other outstanding entrees include a subtly-flavored *escalope de veau moutarde de meaux* and supreme of chicken princess with asparagus (see following recipes). Roast prime rib of beef with freshly-baked pop-over is offered frequently as a special item. Among the appetizers are clams Casino (of course), escargot, littleneck clams and French onion soup au gratin. An ample and changing selection of desserts is available and might include strawberry shortcake, chocolate mousse and a variety of delicious tortes and cakes.

As a unique setting for special occasions, the Canfield House also specializes in catering to groups, parties and weddings.

A welcoming and attractive bar with open fireplace features piano entertainment on weekends and provides a comfortable retreat from the pressures of modern-day life.

It comes as no surprise to learn that the owners of the Canfield House have built up a large local following of people who enjoy the rare experience of fine dining in the atmosphere of an era never likely to return.

THE CANFIELD HOUSE

5 Memorial Boulevard, Newport • (401) 847-0416

OPEN: 5 to 10 p.m.
CLOSED: Mondays
DINNER: from 5 to 10 p.m., Sunday: 3 to 10 p.m.
        (Until 9:00 p.m. off-season)
SEATS: 90
CHILDREN'S PORTIONS: available any time
SEPARATE BAR: open 4 p.m. to 1 a.m.
CREDIT CARDS: CB, DC, MC, VISA
PARKING: ample private parking
RESERVATIONS: advised, call 847-0416

Oysters Rockefeller

16 freshly-shucked oysters on the bottom shell
2 lbs. spinach
2 tablespoons chopped shallots
¼ lb. butter
3 oz. Pernod
Cheddar cheese
Dash of nutmeg
Salt & pepper to taste

Steam spinach in one inch of boiling water. Drain and cool spinach. In a saute pan, glaze shallots in butter. As the shallots become translucent, add the spinach to the pan. Season with salt & pepper, a dash of nutmeg and the Pernod. Blend together over a slow flame.

Top oysters with spinach mixture and a small piece of cheddar cheese. Bake in oven at 375 degrees until cheese melts onto oysters.

Scrod Baked in Flaky Pastry

SERVES 6-8

3 lbs. fresh scrod
1 sheet of puff pastry
2 lbs. spinach
2 lbs. mushrooms
4 or 5 shallots

Prepare spinach — pick and wash thoroughly. Steam spinach, cool and drain off excess water. Saute chopped shallots in butter and add spinach. Season with salt and pepper and a dash of nutmeg. Prepare mushrooms — slice and saute in chopped shallots and butter. Put on one side.

This dish is prepared by rolling out the puff pastry into a large square. The spinach is spread thinly and completely across the pastry dough. Next, the mushrooms are spread across the spinach layer. The fresh scrod is then centered on the mushroom layer, and the dough is carefully wrapped around the fish.

The pastry can be sealed by wetting the edges with an egg wash (eggs lightly beaten with milk). To bring out the color of the pastry, coat the dough with egg wash using a pastry brush. Bake scrod in oven at 375 degrees until browned.

To serve, cut a slice of pastry and turn portions on their side on the plate to show a center of white fish surrounded by a ring of mushrooms, a ring of spinach and a layer of pastry.

Monkfish Tails en Piperade SERVES 6

Monkfish is a good resource in these days of inflation and scarcity. It is a cook's delight because it is so adaptable; its firm texture suits it to many dishes and its mild flavor can be enhanced with spices and sauces. Be sure to cut and peel off the grayish membrane covering the outer side of the fillet if the fish market has not done so.

The Piperade Mixture:

2 large green bell peppers
2 large red bell peppers
1 large yellow onion
2 tablespoons or so of olive oil
2 or 3 cloves of garlic, pureed
1 teaspoon of mixed Italian herbs
¼ teaspoon or so of salt
freshly-ground black pepper

The Fish and other ingredients:

3½ lbs. monkfish fillets
1 cup dry white wine
1 cup fish or chicken broth
2 tablespoons or so of olive oil
salt and pepper
flour

Halve, stem and seed the peppers. Cut into very fine long, thin slices. Peel the onion, halve, and cut into thin lengthwise slices. Cook the vegetables in olive oil in a large frying pan over moderate heat for 4 or 5 minutes. Add the herbs, garlic and seasonings. The vegetables should be only partially cooked.

Cut the fish into serving-size pieces. Dredge lightly in the flour which has been seasoned with salt and pepper. Heat oil over moderate heat in a frying pan until it is very hot, but not smoking. Add the fish in one layer. Saute until fish stiffens slightly — do not brown.

Spread the vegetables over the fish. Pour in the wine and broth. Cover and simmer for about 10 minutes. The fish is cooked when it has turned from springy to gently soft. It needs a little more cooking than other fish, but be sure not to overcook it to a point where it falls apart.

Arrange the fish and vegetables on a hot platter and cover. Rapidly boil down the juices until almost syrupy, spoon over the fish and serve.

Steak and Kidney Pie

SERVES 4

1 small onion
2 carrots
1 lb. sirloin
1 lb. fresh lamb kidneys
1 tablespoon tomato paste
2 cups jus de veau
6 tablespoons Worcestershire sauce
salt and pepper to taste

Chop onion and carrots finely. Glaze onions and carrots in saute pan until soft.
    Cube sirloin and kidneys. Dredge in flour and sear in hot butter. Combine
vegetables with sirloin and kidneys. Season with salt and pepper. Add tomato
paste, Worcestershire sauce and jus de veau. Simmer slowly for 10 minutes.
Place in casserole dish and top with puff pastry. Bake in oven at 400 degrees
for 15 minutes.

Chicken Princess

SERVES 4

4 boneless, skinless breasts of chicken,
    about 8 oz. each
8 spears white asparagus
2 cups chicken sauce
egg wash: 4 eggs lightly beaten with ½ cup milk
approx. 8 cups fine white breadcrumbs
flour seasoned with salt and pepper
clarified margarine

Dredge the chicken pieces in seasoned flour. Place each one in the egg wash
to coat, then into the breadcrumbs. Pat the chicken on both sides with a dry
hand to lightly coat with the crumbs.
    Heat the margarine in a large frying pan until it is almost smoking. Brown
the chicken pieces lightly on both sides. Place them on a baking sheet and
bake in the oven at 350 degrees until tender (about 10 minutes).
    While the chicken is baking, warm asparagus spears in a little water in
a saucepan.
    To serve: place 2 spears of asparagus on each chicken breast and ribbon
with chicken sauce.

Veal Moutarde de Meaux

SERVES 4

4 6-oz. veal cutlets
1⅓ cups heavy cream
4 tablespoons Moutarde de Meaux mustard
1 tablespoon clarified butter
salt and freshly-ground pepper

Heat butter in a skillet. Pass veal through flour and place in hot butter. Cook lightly without coloring, then cook other side.

Add cream and Moutarde de Meaux. Mix with the back of a wooden spoon over a gentle flame for two minutes. Place veal on a platter and spoon sauce over the cutlets.

Pears Poached in White Wine

SERVES 12

6 pears of the Anjou, Bartlett or Comice size,
   ripe and unblemished

   Poaching syrup:

3 cups dry white wine, preferably dry white
   French vermouth
1 cup water
zest of 1 lemon and 4 tablespoons of lemon juice
1 stick or ½ teaspoon powdered cinnamon
1½ cups sugar

Choose a saucepan that will be large enough to hold the pears submerged in the syrup. Place the syrup ingredients in the pan and bring to a simmer; simmer for 5 minutes and then remove from heat.

One by one, working quickly, peel the pears and slip them into the syrup. When all the pears are peeled, bring the syrup barely to a simmer and maintain at this temperature for 8 or 10 minutes, until the pears are tender through when pierced with the sharp point of a small knife.

When done, cover pan and leave the pears to absorb the flavors of the syrup for 20 minutes. (The pears can be held covered and refrigerated in the syrup for several days.)

To serve: carefully slice each pear in half lengthwise and core. Place each half in a bowl with some of the syrup; you may wish to add heavy cream or top with whipped cream.

SALAS'

Salas' is a fun place to visit, as well as being one of the best food bargains in the area. Here you'll rub shoulders with hungry fishermen, local residents, boisterous yachting crews, penny-wise students and canny tourists, all enjoying Salas' far-reaching reputation for serving generous portions of quality food at stay-at-home prices.

Founded in 1952 by Maria and Francisco Salas with a $150 loan from Maria's father, Salas' is genuinely a family business. Francisco is from Guam and met Maria while he was cooking for the Navy in Newport. Sons Rick and Frank are managers, and various other relatives help out in the kitchens, dining rooms and the two bars.

The menu is a collection of unusual, even eccentric, items, loosely grouped into four basic categories. First there's Italian food, including spaghetti which is sold by weight (in quarter pound, half pound or pound servings); there's fresh local seafood—the Salas' Clambake, available in two versions, is a real feast: No. 1 comes with a lobster, clams, sausage, fish, corn-on-the-cob, onion, potato, broth and drawn butter; and No. 2 includes clams, sausage, chourico (Portuguese sausage), fish, onion, potato, corn-on-the-cob, frankfurter, broth and drawn butter. Salas' provides a good selection of choice steaks, served with salad and potato (they claim no responsibility for steaks well-done). And last but certainly not least, comes Salas' infamous Oriental Spaghetti, an obscure specialty from Guam. You may choose from chicken, pork or shrimp (see following recipe), with fried rice as an accompaniment. A small but well-rounded wine list complements this varied selection of food, and the Salas' pina colada has been reported to be the best in New England—Maria says she got the "secret recipe" from a bartender in Puerto Rico many years ago.

The atmosphere here can be frenetic—this may not be *quite* the spot for an intimate dinner for two. The decor is authentic Victorian — the building, dating from the mid 1800's, was originally a bank, and later a general store; the heavy oak staircase is still in place, and oak wainscoting and tin ceilings and walls are in evidence in various rooms. Despite the dignified surroundings, the atmosphere is casual and carefree, the background music comprising mostly of the laughter of contented diners.

Downstairs, The **Brasserie at Salas'** serves much the same menu as upstairs but with additional nightly specials. However, Salas' famous Oriental Spaghetti is only available upstairs. The adjacent **Raw Bar & Seafood Deli** at Salas' is a no-nonsense deli featuring fresh seafood — lobsters, crabs, stuffed quahogs — as well as pasta, salads and chowder. All items are available for take-out, or you may prefer to rollup your sleeves and dine royally on a paper plate right there with a pitcher of beer to wash it down.

Salas' is a popular congregating spot, but please note they do *not* take reservations, so make sure you get there early as the line can sometimes spill downstairs out into the street. But even so, the wait's always worth it.

SALAS' DINING ROOM
341 - 343 Thames Street, Newport • (401) 846-8772

OPEN: seven days a week, year 'round
  except Thanksgiving & Christmas
DINNER: 4:00—10:00 p.m.
SEATS: 86
CHILDREN'S PORTIONS: not served
CREDIT CARDS: AMEX, CB, DC, MC, VISA
PARKING: limited
RESERVATIONS: NOT accepted

THE BRASSERIE AT SALAS'
(401) 849-7895

OPEN: seven days a week May—Sept.
DINNER: 6:00—10:00 p.m.
SEATS: 60
CREDIT CARDS: AMEX, CB, DC, MC, VISA
RESERVATIONS: NOT accepted

UNITED STATES
POSTAL SERVICE.
NORTHEAST AREA

POSTAL CUSTOMER

Dear Postal Customer:

The National Association of Letter Carriers, in conjunction with the U.S. Postal Service, the AFL-CIO and the United Way of America, will be collecting nonperishable food items on May 13 for distribution to food banks in our community.

Please place a food donation by your mailbox on Saturday, May 13. Your letter carrier will pick it up and deliver it to the food bank. Help us to help our community.

Thank You,

Your Letter Carrier

THE FAMILY CIRCUS®

© 1995 BKI

Bil Keane

SATURDAY, MAY 13

Oriental Spaghetti with Pork

1 lb. box linguine
1 lb. pork cut into strips, tenderloin if available
½ onion, medium to large, cut into strips
½ stalk celery, sliced into small pieces
1 large green pepper, sliced into strips
½ cup soy sauce
2 pinches Accent
¼ teaspoon garlic powder
1 scallion stalk

Pre-cook linguine as directed on box, then rinse. Add a little oil to the pasta, toss, and refrigerate.

In a large frying pan or a wok cook the pork strips slowly. When the pork is thoroughly cooked, add celery, onions and green peppers. Toss and cook briefly — the vegetables must stay crisp. Reduce heat a little and add linguine, soy sauce, Accent and garlic powder, continually tossing until all ingredients are blended well and the cooked linguine is heated through.

Garnish with chopped scallions and serve immediately with soy sauce on the side for those who prefer more.

The Brasserie's Marinated Chicken

6 chicken halves
8 cups soy sauce
8 cups water
4 cloves garlic, crushed
Juice from one large lemon
1 large onion, chopped
¾ cup sesame oil
8 tablespoons brown sugar
1 tablespoon powdered ginger
⅓ cup white vinegar
1 pinch white pepper

Mix all ingredients in a large container, cover and refrigerate overnight.

Preheat oven to 400 degrees. Bake chicken for about 45 minutes to one hour until done. Spanish-style rice is a good accompaniment for this dish.

Baked Scallops

SERVES 4

**2 lb. sea scallops, cut into bite-sized pieces
  and rinsed well
3 tablespoons cooking sherry
Juice from ½ lemon
2 pinches Accent
¼ teaspoon onion powder
¼ teaspoon garlic powder
1 pinch white pepper
½ teaspoon paprika**

Mix sherry, lemon juice, Accent, onion powder, garlic powder, white pepper and paprika in a large bowl. Toss in scallops, cover and refrigerate for several hours of marinating time. Pre-heat oven to 450 degrees.

Place scallops in individual oven-proof baking dishes. Do not add too much liquid when placing scallops in the baking dishes as they release a lot of juice as they cook. After about 8 minutes cooking time, toss scallops around for even cooking. Sprinkle bread crumbs on top, dot with butter and return to the oven for about another 5 minutes or until the topping is browned. Serve with fresh parsley sprigs and lemon wedges.

Breadcrumb Topping

**½ cup fresh bread crumbs
4 tablespoons melted butter
Juice of 1/8 of a small lemon
½ teaspoon paprika
2 dashes cooking sherry**

Mix all ingredients well.

SALAS'

Grilled Shrimp and Italian Sausage

SERVES 4

⅓ cup olive oil
Juice of ¼ lemon
1 clove garlic, crushed
2 leaves fresh basil
1 bay leaf
2 pinches salt
1 pinch white pepper
16 shrimp, U 15 or jumbo, shelled and deveined
11 Italian sausages
8 wooden skewers

Precook the sausages and set them aside to cool.

Cut the shrimp in half down the back and place them in a bowl. Add the rest of the ingredients, toss well and marinate for at least an hour. Soak the skewers in water so they will not burn on the grill.

When the sausages are cool, cut each one into three pieces. The next procedure may be tricky but creates an attractive presentation. Take one of the shrimp halves and place one end on a skewer. Then put a piece of sausage on the skewer and wrap the other end of the shrimp around the sausage and onto the skewer, making a crescent shape. Put four shrimp and four pieces of sausage on each skewer; two skewers make a serving. Place these on a hot Hibachi or a charcoal barbecue grill. Turn occasionally for even cooking. When the shrimp are firm and dark around the edges they are ready to serve (do not overcook or the shrimp will become dry).

LA PETITE AUBERGE

The charming French restaurant **La Petite Auberge** was opened in 1976 by Roger and Martine Putier. The Putiers hail from Lyon, capital of French gastronomy, where Roger received his classical training; later he served General de Gaulle as Maitre d' for three years. With such a background it is little wonder that the owners of La Petite Auberge have succeeded in creating an authentic French country inn in the heart of downtown Newport, just off Washington Square.

The interior seems more like a private home than a restaurant. The layout of the old Colonial building, noted as being the birthplace of Stephen Decatur, has been left intact so dining rooms are small and intimate. They are decorated romantically in soft blue and grey downstairs; pale green and gold upstairs. Thick carpeting, floor-length jacquard curtains and antique furniture and paintings set the scene for exquisite table settings with white lace coverings over blue or green linen tablecloths, fan-fashioned matching napkins and fresh flowers.

The dinner menu offers an interesting selection of classic dishes including beef Wellington with truffle sauce, chicken Charles V with apples and cognac (see following recipe), lobster tails in champagne sauce, and both chicken and veal prepared *a la Petite Auberge* — with morels and cream sauce. For dessert there's creme caramel, strawberries Romanoff, cherries jubilee, banana flambe, and (heaven on earth!) crepes Suzette. Specialties of the house include escargots Petite Auberge (with cepes), clams a la facon du chef, and duck with raspberries (see recipe). After dinner, try a cafe flambe maison—coffee flamed with brandy, cream of cocoa and coffee brandy.

La Petite Auberge is dedicated to those who love gourmet food or who are willing to learn to appreciate it. "Freshness and honesty" is the philosophy of the kitchen, and there one might add "wizardry", considering the culinary feats that are performed night after night in the pint-sized kitchen.

Guests may also dine outside in the tiny rose garden, shielded from the narrow street by a trellis. On the far side of this courtyard is an adjoining bar, **Le Cafe;** with its rustic brick floor, open fireplace and plain wooden tables, it's a perfect place for less formal dining or an after-dinner drink.

Known as one of the best French restaurants in New England, La Petite Auberge stirs distant memories of great meals in provincial France, and promises many more right here in Newport.

LA PETITE AUBERGE
19 Charles Street, Newport • (401) 849-6669

OPEN: seven days a week, year 'round
DINNER: 6:00 to 10:00 p.m.
SEATS: 48
BAR: Le Cafe, same hours as dining room
CHILDREN'S PORTIONS: available on special request only
CREDIT CARDS: AMEX, DC, MC, VISA
PARKING: no private lot but parking available around building
RESERVATIONS: advised

Fish Pernod

2 filets white fish
1 cup milk
1 cup flour
1 oz. margarine
2 tablespoons oil
salt and white pepper
Pernod

Any local white fish will do — cod, scrod, blackfish, etc.

Place milk and flour in separate dishes or soup plates. Place each filet of fish in milk and then in flour. Saute in margarine and oil. Season with salt and white pepper. When cooked, place fish in a serving dish and dot with sweet butter. Flame with Pernod. Garnish with lemon and parsley and serve.

Darne of Salmon La Petite Auberge

1 salmon steak per person
1 or 2 cups milk
salt & white pepper
thyme
1 bay leaf
1 oz. butter
½ oz. or so pink peppercorns
½ cup shallots, chopped
½ cup or so Madeira wine
1 pint heavy cream

Take one darne (approximately 1 in. thick salmon steak) per person. Poach in milk with salt, white pepper, thyme and a bay leaf. Cook for approximately 5 to 7 minutes, or when the bone of the salmon can be easily removed.

In another saucepan saute pink peppercorns and chopped shallots in butter. Add Madeira wine and reduce with about one pint of heavy cream until thick. Season to taste.

Remove outer skin and bone from salmon. Pour sauce over salmon and serve immediately.

Duck with Raspberries
A La Facon Du Chef

SERVES 4

1 duck
raspberry vinegar
3 tablespoons honey
½ pint duck sauce (see following recipe)
fresh raspberries

Roast the duck; chef recommends that cooking the duck one day in advance gives best results.

Split duck down the middle and remove all bones inside. Separate the duck breast from the wings. Wrap portions in aluminum foil and place in oven for 15 to 20 minutes at 375 degrees. This removes excess grease and makes sure the duck is dry.

Deglaze the pan the duck was cooked in with raspberry vinegar and reduce. Add around 3 tablespoons of honey and ½ pint of duck sauce. Cook until it boils. Unwrap duck portions and place on serving dish. Garnish with fresh raspberries in season, or raspberries with natural syrup. Pour sauce over duck and serve.

Duck Sauce

1 cup sugar
3 cups vinegar
bones from duck
1 orange, squeezed
2 cups orange juice
½ gallon water

Reduce one cup sugar with 3 cups regular vinegar until syrup is formed — do not let the mixture carmelize. Mix in remaining bones from the duck with 1 squeezed orange, 2 cups orange juice and ½ gallon of water. Cook slowly until sauce reduces to half volume.

Le Poulet Charles V

SERVES 4—6

1 chicken, 3 to 4 lbs.
4 apples
a splash of brandy
3 tablespoons white wine
beurre manie

Roast a chicken for about 30 minutes. Peel, core and slice 4 apples and add to the pan and roast until the chicken is cooked.

Remove chicken and apples from pan, leaving a small amount of grease. Flame the pan with brandy, then add about 3 tablespoons white wine with a little water and bring to a boil. Add a little *beurre manie* and mix in to thicken sauce. Pour sauce over chicken and apple slices and serve.

Beurre Manié (Butter with flour)

1 stick sweet butter or margarine
½ to 1 cup flour

Melt one stick of sweet butter or margarine. Mix with ½ to 1 cup flour. Use small pellets for thickening any sauce quickly, but do not let sauce boil after adding it. Can be stored in refrigerator.

Parfait La Petite Auberge

3 scoops coffee ice cream
2 tablespoons Grand Marnier
1 tablespoon Kirsch
whipped cream

Place three scoops of coffee ice cream in a glass dish or a tall glass. Pour over 2 tablespoons Grand Marnier and 1 tablespoon Kirsch. Top with fresh whipped cream.

Please call La Petite Auberge at (401) 849-6669 if you have any questions about these recipes.

THE PIER

The Pier was recently voted the top restaurant in the state for business dining, and with good reason — the simple formula for the restaurant's success, according to Mrs. Enid Bucci, one of the owners, is serving generous portions of freshly-cooked food at sensible prices.

The idea for a restaurant in this location was conceived in 1964 by David Rocklin, owner of the Williams & Manchester Shipyard (home of the 12 metre yacht Freedom, victorious defender of the 1980 America's Cup Series). He rightly reasoned that, since the activity and equipment of the boatyard fascinated him, it was sure to interest a lot of other people as well, and attract them to a waterfront restaurant in a part of Newport which at that time was not very fashionable. The venture was an instant success, and by 1969 the restaurant had become so popular that the dining rooms were expanded to handle twice the original seating capacity. Leonard "Buck" Ossick became a partner in the early days on the strength of 30 years experience in the restaurant business and still manages things at The Pier today. Four years after David Rocklin died in 1963, Fred Bucci became the business manager for the restaurant when he married the former Mrs. Rocklin.

As would be expected, the decor, like the view, is distinctly nautical. Old barn boards from Vermont panel the dining rooms and lounge, creating an informal backdrop for an antique grandfather clock, boating memorabilia, sturdy tables and gleaming glassware. For summer guests, there's a deck outdoors overlooking the water where patrons can sit and order a drink while waiting for their table for lunch or dinner. The food is a diversified selection of fresh seafood supplied by local fishing boats, charcoal-broiled steaks, chops, roast beef and duckling. For a memorable meal, start with a tasty bowl of Yankee fish chowder (see recipe), or clams casino, then tackle The Pier's bountiful clambake with all the trimmings . . . and, if you've got room, order The Pier ice cream pie (see recipe) for a delicious dessert to round off the meal.

The Pier has always appealed to a broad spectrum of clientele — yachtsmen and naval officers, fishermen and businessmen, families and young singles — all endorsing the owner's original philosophy that fine food, reasonable prices, generous portions and drinks that are "free-poured" will bring customers back time and again.

THE PIER
West Howard Wharf, Newport • (401) 849-3100

OPEN: seven days a week, all year
LUNCH: Noon to 3:00 p.m.
DINNER: 5:00 to 10:30 p.m.
SANDWICHES: always available in the bar
SEATS: 275, including lounge
CHILDREN'S PORTIONS: available
PRIVATE DINING ROOM AND BAR: available for parties —
   group menus available
CREDIT CARDS: American Express, The Pier's own credit card
PARKING: ample
RESERVATIONS: advised, call 847-3645 or 849-3100

Yankee Fish Chowder

YIELD: 8 bowls

2 tablespoons butter
1 clove garlic, minced
1 onion, diced
1 green pepper, diced
1 rib celery, diced
8 oz. crushed tomatoes
8 oz. Burgundy wine
1 lb. filet of cod
3 cups diced potatoes
6 cups water
Salt to taste
Worcestershire sauce
Tabasco sauce
White pepper

Melt butter in pot, add onion, green pepper, celery and garlic and saute until tender, stirring frequently; do not brown. Add water, crushed tomatoes, cod, Burgundy, and diced potatoes. Season with white pepper, salt, Tabasco sauce and Worcestershire sauce. Bring to boil and cook until the potatoes and fish are tender.

Brussels Sprouts Au Gratin

SERVES 6

2 lbs. Brussels sprouts
1 oz. dry mustard
4 oz. sharp cheese
1 quart cream sauce
Parmesan cheese
Cracker crumbs
Salt and pepper to taste

Bring the Brussels sprouts to a a boil, stir and cook for one more minute. Drain and place in a shallow baking pan. Add dry mustard, salt and pepper. Break the sharp cheese into 1 quart of cream sauce and let it melt. Pour over the sprouts and mix well. Top with cracker crumbs and Parmesan cheese. Dot with butter and bake for 35 — 40 minutes at 400 degrees.

Filet of Sole Stuffed with Lobster

SERVES 8

2 lbs. fresh lobster meat
2 lbs. filet of sole
8 oz. butter
Cracker crumbs

Preheat oven to 400 degrees. Melt butter. Cut lobster meat into bite-sized pieces. Portion eight 4 oz. servings on a sheet pan, forming each into a mound. Cover the lobster meat with the filet of sole, placing the skin side of the fish down. Sprinkle cracker crumbs over the sole, just enough to lightly coat. Liberally moisten each portion with the melted butter. Add a cup of water to the pan and place in oven at 400 degrees for 20 minutes or until fish is done,

Remove from pan with spatula and place on serving plate. Top with "The Pier" Newburg sauce:

Newburg Sauce

YIELD: 2½ cups

4 tablespoons butter
4 tablespoons flour
2 cups cream
1 tablespoon paprika
4 tablespoons dry sherry
Salt
White pepper
Dry mustard
Tabasco sauce
Lea & Perrins Worcestershire Sauce

Melt the butter in a thick saucepan and gradually add the flour, stirring constantly over a low flame for 3 to 5 minutes. Gradually add 2 cups of scalded cream, stirring constantly with a wire whisk to blend well.

Season to taste with salt, white pepper and dry mustard. Add two dashes of Tabasco sauce, two dashes Worcestershire sauce and one tablespoon paprika. Finish by adding the dry sherry and whip together for 5 minutes over a very low flame.

Pier Ice Cream Pie

¼ cup melted butter
1¼ cups Graham cracker crumbs
⅓ cup water
1 large Hershey almond chocolate bar
1 pint coffee ice cream
1 pint chocolate ice cream
Whipped cream

Press 1¼ cups Graham cracker crumbs mixed with ¼ cup melted butter firmly into 9½" pie plate. Bake at 350 degrees for 8 minutes. Cool.

Melt one large Hershey almond chocolate bar with ⅓ cup water. Pour over cooled crust and freeze.

Bring 1 pint each of chocolate and coffee ice cream to room temperature. Spread chocolate ice cream over chocolate crust. Spread coffee ice cream over chocolate ice cream. Freeze.

Serve with whipped cream.

Banana Taster   SERVES 4

4 tablespoons butter
¼ cup packed brown sugar
½ teaspoon cinnamon
2 tablespoons banana liqueur
4 medium-sized firm bananas,
      halved lengthwise and cut crosswise
¼ cup Mount Gay rum
4 scoops vanilla ice cream

Melt butter in a skillet. Add sugar, cinnamon and banana liqueur; stir to mix. Bring to boil and simmer for two minutes. Place bananas in sauce. Cook, stirring occasionally, until bananas are soft, about four miñutes. Add rum; allow to heat slightly. Ignite.

Serve over vanilla ice cream.

Zabaglione

½ cup Marsala wine
3 tablespoons sugar
4 egg yolks
Pinch of salt
A few drops of vanilla flavoring
1 pint strawberries
Cinnamon

Combine wine and sugar in the top of a double boiler. Place over simmering water (upper pan should not touch water). Add egg yolks and salt. Using wire whisk, beat until mixture thickens and mounds, about 8 minutes. Beat in vanilla.

Serve in a tall glass over strawberries and sprinkle lightly with cinnamon. May be served with waffles if desired.

MURIEL'S

Muriel's will charm you with its cozy surroundings, friendly atmosphere and home-cooked food at affordable prices. Founder Muriel M. Barclay de Tolly, a long-time Newport resident, opened her namesake restaurant in the center of Newport in 1986. A natural cook armed with an impressive collection of family recipes, Muriel realized opening her own restaurant would be a challenge but felt that her love of people would greatly increase her chance of success. She invited her son, Paul, a mechanical engineer and cabinet maker, to join her in this enterprise, and he designed and rebuilt the restaurant's attractive interior. Together they've created a friendly and whimsical place which combines a fresh contemporary look with Victorian charm. A collection of colorful Maxfield Parrish prints are perfectly offset by teal-colored walls, and this color scheme is picked up in the floral tablecloths covered by lace squares under plate glass. Lacy curtains veil the windows from the street, while smart striped awnings shade the windows outside. This decor sets the scene for an amusing design accent—a couple of immaculately-dressed mannequins are posed at various spots around the restaurant, perhaps seated at the piano, or under a potted palm.

Muriel's stands on its reputation for serving good food prepared to order with strictly fresh ingredients. Dishes range from down-home favorites to more sophisticated and contemporary selections, and include some interesting salads and stir-fry dishes (choice of chicken, jumbo shrimp, beef or scallops) in accordance with the current trend towards lighter fare. Desserts, however, make no concession to current culinary fashion and include such homemade favorites as raisin bread pudding with butter rum-raisin sauce (see following recipe), chocolate bread pudding with ice cream and chocolate sauce, strawberry or blueberry shortcake, and carrot cake.

This is a restaurant for all seasons and all times of day—breakfast, lunch and dinner. Breakfast especially is a real treat at Muriel's. Served from 8 to 11:30 weekdays and 9 to 2:00 p.m. on Sunday, it features *huevos rancheros,* Eggs Benedict, pan-fried omelettes, and Belgian waffles with fruit and yogurt, all accompanied by home-baked muffins and pastries. For lunch there's a wide selection of salads, crepes and sandwiches, while dinner features seafood ranging from shrimp Louisiana, sauteed with broccoli, red peppers, mushrooms and onions in a Cajun-spiced wine sauce over fettucine, to scallops Provencal and fish and chips made with Muriel's special beer batter. There are also chicken dishes, pasta, and, for meat eaters, filet mignon with Muriel's bearnaise sauce, and broiled pork chops with sauteed cinnamoned apples and spices. And last, but certainly not least, is Muriel's famous seafood chowder, winner of the Schweppes/Mott New England Chowder Cook-off for two years.

The corner building that houses Muriel's is a bit of an oddity—it's actually a colonial building that was raised one story to allow a store to be built below. Muriel and Paul have turned this compact corner location to their advantage, and have created a restaurant that exudes warmth and exhibits a quirky sense of style. Be warned though that Muriel's has no liquor license so be prepared and B.Y.O.B.

Muriel's Restaurant
Corner of Spring & Touro Streets, Newport • (401) 849-7780

OPEN: all year
CLOSED: Sunday nights off-season
BREAKFAST: Monday through Saturday, 8–11:30 am
LUNCH: Monday through Saturday, 11:30 am–2 pm
DINNER: 5–10 pm
SUNDAY BRUNCH: 9 am–2 pm
BAR: No liquor license, bring your own.
SEATS: 65
CHILDREN'S PORTIONS: available on request
CREDIT CARDS: MC, VISA
PARKING: at Washington Square or municipal lot
    behind movie theatres
RESERVATIONS: call 847-7780

Cheddar and Sausage Soup SERVES 6 to 8

1 gallon half-and-half
½ lb. grated Cheddar cheese
1 whole Kielbasa sausage, chopped
2 cups mushrooms, sliced and sauteed
2 tablespoons chicken base
½ cup butter or margarine
2 tablespoons salt
1 tablespoon pepper
1 tablespoon chopped parsley
½ small onion, grated

Place all the ingredients into a double boiler and heat. When mixture is very hot, add roux (1 cup flour and 2 cups half-and-half, mixed well). Stir well. Cook for another ½ hour on lower heat before serving.

Salmon Steak SERVES 6

6 salmon steaks
3 tomatoes, peeled and cubed
1 green pepper, chopped
pinch of thyme
pinch of chopped scallions
2 mint leaves, chopped
1 cup plain yogurt
1 teaspoon mustard seed
juice of ½ lemon
salt and pepper
pinch of cumin
pinch of cayenne pepper

Sprinkle each steak sparingly with lemon juice, salt, cumin, cayenne pepper and a little oil. Broil 6 to 8 minutes.

To make the sauce: cook 1 teaspoon mustard seed in a little oil. Add the cubed tomatoes, chopped green pepper, pinch of thyme, scallions, mint, and a pinch of pepper. Cook for a few minutes and add one cup of plain yogurt. Stir to heat through and serve over the salmon.

Chicken Teriyaki

SERVES 4

2 lbs. boneless breast of chicken

Marinade:
½ cup peanut oil
½ cup soy sauce
2 tablespoons fresh ginger, peeled and grated
2 garlic cloves, chopped
2 tablespoons orange juice
¼ cup sherry
¼ cup brown sugar

Mix together ingredients for the marinade. Arrange chicken pieces in a ceramic dish and cover with marinade. Let stand overnight in the refrigerator.

Prepare grill or broiler and cook chicken 8 to 10 inches from heat. Cook 7 to 8 minutes on each side while basting well. Serve over wild rice and garnish with wedges of fresh pineapple.

Ginger Chicken

SERVES 4

4 boneless chicken breasts, cut into bite-size pieces
1 stick butter
1 tablespoon freshly-grated ginger
2 bunches scallions, chopped
1 cup chicken stock
2 cans water chestnuts
1 lb. mushrooms, sliced
2 cups sour cream
salt and pepper to taste

Heat butter in a skillet and saute ginger and scallions. Add chicken stock and bring to near boiling point. Add the chicken pieces and reduce heat. Simmer until chicken is just cooked, approximately 8 minutes.

Add water chestnuts, mushrooms, salt and pepper and simmer for a further 2 minutes. Add 2 cups sour cream and cook on a low flame, stirring well. Serve over wild rice garnished with a dab of sour cream on each portion.

Vanilla Bread Pudding with Butter Rum Sauce

SERVES 8

6 eggs
2 cups milk
½ lb. sugar
2 teaspoons ground cinnamon
½ cup raisins
2 teaspoons vanilla extract
1 loaf French bread, approximately
½ cup walnuts
½ cup brown sugar

In a large bowl, mix together the eggs, milk, sugar, cinnamon and raisins. Cut up enough French bread in small cubes to absorb the mixture. Pour mixture into a greased deep baking pan and top with ½ cup walnuts and ½ cup brown sugar. Bake in oven for 45 minutes at 350 degrees.

Butter Rum Sauce:

½ cup melted butter
¾ cup powdered sugar
¼ cup Meyer's rum

Combine all ingredients and cook over medium heat for 15 minutes.

To serve: cut bread pudding into squares and serve warm topped with heated rum sauce.

THE CLARKE COOKE HOUSE

The Clarke Cooke House restaurant is located in an historic three story Colonial manor house on Bannister's Wharf in Newport's bustling waterfront district. The owner restored the building in 1973 and continued to develop Bannister's Wharf, which now includes a marina, twenty stores and ten guest rooms.

The elegant candlelit dining rooms, decorated with period antiques, 18th century oil paintings and charming table settings, provide a soothing atmosphere for the serious work of sampling the myriad delights of the menu. Old wooden staircases connect the different levels of the dining areas and bare floorboards hint at the rustic origins of this historic old building which now houses one of Newport's most sophisticated dining spots.

The restaurant harvests its own vegetables and fruits and raises lamb and pheasant on its farm in nearby Portsmouth. The Chef is constantly striving to serve the very best — his interpretations of the French classics are innovative and inspired by Roger Verge, under whom he studied. You may be struck with agonizing indecision when studying the sumptuous menu (in French with English subtitles) — to make choosing even more difficult, a note on the dinner menu states that the chef will be pleased to prepare any dish you may desire given proper notice. Appetizers include fresh pasta, lobster bisque, carpaccio of lamb, and a smoked salmon salad with caviar egg en cocotte (see recipe); a few selections from the magnificent dinner menu are grilled swordfish with buckwheat fettucine, fricasee de ris de veau, roast rack of lamb persillade (see recipe), a classic entrecote au poivre, and breast of pheasant in cider sauce with a petite ragout and foie gras (see recipe). Finish off the meal with a delicious dessert like crepes Normande with calvados cream, or choose from a cheeseboard of choice imported cheeses. Behind lock and key in an 18th century wine cellar reconstructed in the lower dining room is a fine selection of domestic and European wines. The house wine is specially bottled in Bordeaux for the Clarke Cooke House by Andre Quancard.

The adjacent **Candy Store Cafe** overlooking the harbor serves lunch and dinner in a less formal atmosphere. Cocktails are also served on the outdoor verandas, famous for their exceptional panoramic views of the waterfront.

At the Clarke Cooke House the standards are high and the quality remarkably consistent. Some idea of the care and creativity that go into the preparation of the food can be gauged by glancing at the following recipes. The Clarke Cooke House well deserves its many accolades and offers one of the most memorable dining experiences in Newport.

THE CLARKE COOKE HOUSE
Bannister's Wharf, Newport • (401) 849-2900

OPEN: 11:30 a.m. to 1:00 a.m.
CLARKE COOKE HOUSE: 6:00 to 10:00 p.m., 10:30 weekends and
    holidays. November through April, Saturdays 6:00 to 10:00 p.m.
CANDY STORE CAFE: 11:30 a.m. to 1:00 a.m.
LUNCH & SUPPER: May–Oct. 11:30 a.m. to 10:30 p.m.
    November–April, Wed. through Sunday, 4:30 to 10:00 p.m.
SUNDAY BRUNCH: 11:30 to 3:00 p.m.
SEPARATE BARS: The Candy Store Cafe, the Midway and Skybar,
    overlooking the Harbor; The Daisy, a discotheque
SEATS: 300
CHILDREN'S PORTIONS: available on request
CREDIT CARDS: AMEX, MC, VISA
PARKING: no private lot, but ample parking nearby
RESERVATIONS: advised, 849-2900

Royal Nova Scotia Smoked Salmon Salad, Egg En Cocotte

SERVES 4

The smoked salmon served at the Clarke Cooke House and her sister restaurant Locke-Ober, in Boston, is from Tangiers, Nova Scotia. The Queen of England has also commissioned this smoke house to supply Buckingham Palace. The unique blending of two old world techniques gives this smoked wild salmon a distinctive and refined flavor.

¾ lb. of smoked salmon
1 head of endive
1 leek
½ cup olive oil
1 tbsp. good cider vinegar
1 oz. Sevruga caviar
1 bunch chives, chopped
4 eggs and 4 cocotte molds
1 tbsp. butter

Beurre Blanc:

¼ cup dry white wine
1 shallot, minced
1 tsp. cider vinegar
Juice of 1 lemon
½ cup heavy cream
¾ lb. butter

First, make the beurre blanc and set aside, in a warm place, until service: Over medium heat, in a heavy sauce pan, reduce the lemon juice, cider vinegar, shallot and white wine by half. Cut the butter into small pices, and over a low heat, slowly whisk it into the reduction until all is incorporated.

Wash the endive and leek, slice into julienne strips, and blanch quickly in boiling water. Refresh in cold water. Toss with the oil and vinegar, season lightly with salt and pepper.

Butter the inside of the cocotte ramekins, or demitasse, and gently crack one egg into each. Cover with a layer of chopped chives, and simmer in a water bath until the eggs have completely set, approximately 8 to 10 minutes.

Place the endive and leek salad in the center of a warm plate, circling it with beurre blanc. Gently remove the egg from the mold by inverting it onto the salad.

Thinly slice the smoked salmon and wrap it in alternating layers to form rose-like flowers. Place one on each plate. Spoon a dollop of Sevruga caviar on top of each egg and serve.

Shellfish Stew: Nage of Shrimp, Scallops and Lobster Sauce

SERVES 4

8 large shrimp, peeled and deveined
1 lb. bay scallops
Meat from two 1¼ lb. lobsters—reserve shells
1 leek
2 tbsp. butter

Sauce:

1 pint heavy cream	1 tomato
1 bottle dry, white wine	2 garlic cloves, chopped
¼ lb. sweet butter	Lobster bodies and shells
1 apple, diced	1 cup Cognac
1 onion, coarsely chopped	

In 1 tablespoon butter, saute the onion, apples, garlic, tomato and lobster bodies and shells for 5 minutes. Add the Cognac and flambe. Add the wine and cream and allow to simmer until reduced by one third. Strain through a food mill, forcing the soft pieces of shell and vegetable through. Again reduce the mixture by one third, season lightly with salt and pepper, and whisk in the remaining butter to thicken.

Cut the leek into ¼ inch wide strips and wash thoroughly. Place the butter into a warm saute pan, add the leek and shrimp and cook slowly for two minutes, add the lobster meat (and the lobster tamale if you choose), then the bay scallops. Cook for two more minutes. Add the sauce and stir, to allow the shell fish juices to emulsify with the lobster sauce. Divide the stew into four bowls and serve with a Chardonnay or white Bordeaux.

Breast of Pheasant in Cider Sauce
with a Petit Ragout & Foie Gras

SERVES 2

Our farm in Portsmouth, R.I., has over twenty acres of orchards, where more than twelve types of fruit are harvested. During the Fall, when the apples are ripe for the cider press, the young pheasants are fattened on corn and apples, ready for the oven.

After the pheasants have hung for one week to mellow and develop flavor, bone out the breast, remove the leg, and bone the thigh of two birds.

Ragout:

½ lb. bacon
1 onion, diced
1 leeks, julienned and washed
Pheasant legs
¼ lb. mushrooms
1 apple, diced
2 cups apple cider
½ bottle red wine
Salt and pepper
⅛ tsp. rosemary
¼ tsp. thyme
1 pinch sage

Sauce:

Pheasant bones
6 shallots, finely chopped
1 quart pheasant or chicken stock
1 pint heavy cream
1 pint apple cider

**4 hexagon shaped butter-cooked croutons spread with
1 oz. each of fresh duck foie gras.**
¼ lb. butter

To make the ragout: cook the bacon and onion in a heavy saucepan until the onion is clear. Add the leek, drumsticks and thighs, stirring until the meat is browned. Add the cider, herbs, apple, mushrooms and wine and cook slowly for one hour. Salt and pepper to taste.

To make the sauce: chop the pheasant carcass into 2 inch pieces and brown all sides in hot oil. Strain off the excess fat. Brown the shallots, then add the chicken or pheasant stock (make from the necks and wings), cream and cider and reduce to 2 cups. Season with salt and pepper, strain and keep warm.

Brown the pheasant breasts in 2 tbsp. of butter and finish by adding the sauce and slowly cooking until the breast is firm to the touch. Remove the breasts and whisk the remaining butter into the sauce. Face the plates with the sauce, place a foie gras crouton at the bottom of each plate and a breast on that. Spoon a small serving of ragout at the top of the plate and serve.

Stuffed Zucchini and Summer Squash Flowers

SERVES 4

Summertime at the Clarke Cooke House is a busy time, and the weather warms the rich soil of our Portsmouth farm to yield an abundance of fresh summer vegetables and herbs. Here is a light but heartwarming dish with Provencal overtones using our mid-summer harvest.

1 red pepper
1 green pepper
1 zucchini
1 summer squash
2 cloves garlic
1 eggplant
2 tomatoes
¼ cup extra virgin olive oil

Cut young zucchini and summer squash while they are still in flower, preferably from your own garden. Gently remove the stamen, and slice this squash in a fan, using the flower end as a hinge. Make a ratatouille: dice the vegetables to a *burnoise,* or tiny confetti, and saute in the olive oil; season to taste with salt and pepper. Allow the mixture to cool, then gently stuff the flowers with it, wrapping the petals around the stuffing. Just before service, steam the flowers for four minutes. Garnish with diced tomato drizzled with olive oil.

Rack of Lamb with Tarragon Glaze

SERVES 4

No dish better describes the cuisine of this restaurant than the lamb that is raised on our farm.

1 hotel rack of lamb, French trim, cut in four portions.

Marinade:

1 quart olive oil
½ head of garlic
4 mint leaves
3 bay leaves
2 lemons, sliced

Sauce:

2 lb. lamb trimmings and bones
4 each: celery stalks, onions, carrots—rough cut
2 heads of garllc
2 tbsp. tomato paste
2 cups Madeira
2 oz. Creme de Menthe
1 tbsp. chopped tarragon
3 tbsp. sweet butter

Garnish:

⅓ cup honey
⅓ cup Pommery mustard
⅓ cup bread crumbs
1 bunch chopped parsley

Marinate lamb for two days.

Brown reserved trimmings and bones in oil. Discard oil and cover bones with 3 quarts of cold water. Add remaining sauce ingredients except the butter. Reduce liquid to one cup and strain.

    Wrap bones of rack of lamb in tin foil to prevent them from being scorched and roast the lamb in a very hot oven (500 degrees) for 8 to 10 minutes (rare to medium rare). Before serving, mix Pommery mustard and honey. Spread on lamb; sprinkle with bread crumbs and parsley and brown under boiler.

    Place the sauce in a sauce pan; whisk in 3 tablespoons of sweet butter. Sauce four warmed plates and place the racks of lamb on the sauce with the foil removed to serve.

Fresh Fruit Torte

1 pint raspberries
6 kiwi fruits, sliced
1 pint strawberries, hulled and sliced lengthways
2 ripe bananas, sliced
1 ripe pineapple, cut into slices
1 jar currant jelly
1 cup Melba sauce
1 cup whipped cream
1 cup crushed almonds, toasted
1 cup Creme Anglaise

2 oz. Grand Marnier
2 oz. Cassis
2 oz. Banana liqueur
2 oz. Amaretto
1 Genoise cake

Cut the Genoise (see following recipe) into four equal sized rectangles. Soak each cake in 2 oz. of one of the above liqueurs.

Place the Grand Marnier-soaked Genoise on a serving dish and place a layer of strawberries upon it. Cover with one cup of Creme Anglaise (see following recipe). Next place the Cassis-soaked Genoise over this layer and add a coating of currant jelly and a layer of raspberries. Cover this with Melba sauce. Place the banana liqueur-soaked Genoise on top and cover with a layer of sliced bananas topped with whipped cream. Next place the Amaretto-soaked Genoise on top, covered with a layer of sliced pineapple slivers. Pipe on the remaining whipped cream and garnish the top of the torte with a line of kiwi fruit, sliced in half and overlapping. Sprinkle with crushed, toasted almonds. Chill and serve.

Genoise:

2½ cups sugar
16 eggs
3½ cups sifted flour
½ lb. sweet butter, clarified

Beat the sugar and eggs for 15 minutes at high speed in an electric mixer. Fold in the sifted flour gently. Pour batter into a rectangular buttered baking sheet pan and bake for 15 minutes in a pre-heated oven at 350 degrees. Allow to cool.

Creme Anglaise:

6 egg yolks
2 oz. Grand Marnier
1 pint heavy cream
½ cup sugar

Beat the ingredients over a double boiler in a stainless steel bowl for 20 minutes or until thick. Cool over an ice bath.

SARDELLA'S

Sardella's is a stylish *trattoria* situated on Memorial Boulevard just a few minute's walk up the hill from the waterfront. Located in the same building where the famous jazz spot *Hurley's* used to be, Sardella's aims to offer fine food in relaxed and attractive surroundings. Custom-made stained glass panels act as room dividers, and the polished wooden floors and elegant table settings give a clean, contemporary look. In summer planters of colorful flowers and greenery, awnings and cafe umbrellas brighten the sidewalk entrance and patio.

Sardella's is one of Newport's most authentic Italian restaurants. Richard Sardella and his chefs have spent time in Italy researching dishes, sampling wines and generally absorbing the friendly atmosphere of the Italian countryside with the intention of duplicating it in their restaurant.

The menu at Sardella's has a wide selection of *antipasti* including *zuppa di frutti di mare* (mediterranean fish soup), *mozzarella in carrozza* (lightly breaded fried cheese served with tomato sauce—see following recipe), *cozze e vino bianco* (mussels steamed in white wine and butter) and snail salad. The dinner selections include homemade ravioli in a basil cream sauce, excellent veal dishes such as Veal Lorretta (scalloppini of veal sauteed in butter with bacon, mushrooms and onions, laced with brandy), and the traditional veal and chicken parmigiana and marsala.

The extensive wine list is one hundred percent Italian and the *vino di casa* (house wines) are served in individual pitchers.

Tucked away at the back of the building is **Salute,** a comfortable bar with a clubby atmosphere. For a special after-dinner drink here try Italian Coffee, made with real whipped cream. As an added diversion in the summer, guests may pass their time playing a game of traditional *bocce* on a court at the side of the building.

Sardella's is a friendly neighborhood meeting place where guests can feel at home and enjoy fine cooking at reasonable prices. If you are looking for a place to enjoy a quiet, romantic dinner, or a leisurely cocktail on a street-side patio, Sardella's is the place.

SARDELLA'S
30 Memorial Boulevard West, Newport • (401) 849-6312

OPEN: all year, 4:00 p.m. − 1:00 a.m. daily
DINNER: 5:00 − 10:00 p.m.
BAR: open 4:00 p.m. − 1:00 a.m.
SEATS: 100
CHILDREN'S PORTIONS: available
CREDIT CARDS: DC, MC, VISA
PARKING: street parking and Almac's parking lot
RESERVATIONS: advised in season

Mozzarella in Carozza

All-cream Mozzarella
Beaten egg
Breadcrumbs
Peanut Oil

This is an Italian form of a "cheese dream". Cut some all-cream Mozzarella into ⅓ inch thick slices, measuring roughly 3 by 2 inches, then dip the pieces into beaten egg. Roll them gently in plain breadcrumbs and let them sit for a few minutes so that the first coating may dry. Then repeat dipping and breading and made sure that the cheese is well sealed on all sides.

Fry cheese in oil (peanut works the best) to a golden brown and serve immediately on a hot plate. Serve with tomato sauce, or for a more pungent treat, make a sauce of four finely chopped cloves of garlic and seven filets of mashed anchovies and simmer in enough oil to liquify.

Cozze e Vino Bianco
(Steamed Mussels)

SERVES 1

Per Person:
18 mussels, medium to large
1 small onion, sliced
1 clove garlic, crushed
½ bay leaf
½ cup white wine
Dash of pepper

Select about 18 mussels, medium to large, and preferably from Maine. Beard them by pulling out the fuzz that keeps them attached to each other. Wash them thorougly and place in a large pot. Slice one small onion per portion, and add to the pot, along with a dash of pepper, a clove of garlic, crushed, half a bay leaf and half a cup of white wine. Cover. Steam until mussels are wide open, about 5 to 7 minutes.

Scaloppine Di Pollo Alla Parmigiana
(Chicken Cutlets Parmesan)

SERVES 2

4 chicken breasts
4 tablespoons butter
Mozzarella cheese
1½ cups tomato sauce
Salt and pepper to taste
Flour
Parmesan cheese

Between sheets of vinyl wrap, pound 8 half chicken breasts to less than ¼ inch thickness. Dry them, season with salt and pepper, dust with flour and saute over a brisk flame in 4 tablespoons of hot butter. They should be brown enough after 2 to 3 minutes of cooking on each side. Arrange the scaloppine in one layer in a flame-proof dish. Place a thick slice of mozzarella cheese on each cutlet, sprinkle with parmesan cheese, and place under a broiler until the cheese melts. Meanwhile, to the pan in which the chicken was sauteed, add 1½ cups of tomato sauce (canned or homemade) and heat it well, stirring in the brown juices from the pan. Serve at once and spoon a ring of sauce around the chicken scaloppine.

Shrimp al Olio

SERVES 4

20 shrimp, U-15
½ cup olive oil
6 anchovy fillets
1-2 cloves garlic, chopped
½ cup clam juice
½ cup white wine
freshly ground black pepper to taste
½ cup parmesan cheese
flour for dredging

Peel and devein shrimp. Chop garlic and anchovies. Heat oil in a large skillet. Dredge shrimp in flour and saute in skillet for one or two minutes on each side. Add garlic and anchovies and simmer until garlic is golden brown. Add white wine and clam juice and bring to a boil. Add a dash of pepper and ½ cup parmesan cheese and serve over pasta.

Pork Tenderloin Moutarde

SERVES 2-3

16 - 24 oz. pork tenderloin
¼ lb. bacon, diced
1 small onion, diced
½ lb. mushrooms, sliced
2 tablespoons Dijon mustard
1½ cups heavy cream, warmed
¼ lb. butter
salt and pepper to taste

Trim pork tenderloin, season and sear on a grill or in a saute pan. Then bake it in the oven for 20 mintues at 325 degrees and let stand.

Saute the bacon in butter until half done. Add diced onions and sliced mushrooms. Saute until onions are transparent. Add mustard and warm cream. Simmer over a low heat, stirring well. Slice pork tenderloin into ¼" to ½" medallions and add to sauce. Simmer until pork reaches desired doneness, and serve.

YESTERDAY'S

Saloons historically have provided a convivial place for people to meet, eat, drink and make merry, and **Yesterday's** follows in this lively tradition. Richard "Biggy" Korn opened Yesterday's in 1974 after ten years in the music and bar business in Newport; he realized there was a need for a hometown saloon/restaurant and was determined to fill the gap. He wanted to establish a place where there would be something for everyone; a place where guests could come in any dress at any time of the day and always find a good variety of delicious food available, from hamburgers and snacks to full dinners. And this is exactly what Yesterday's offers.

The atmosphere is so authentic it's hard to believe the restaurant hasn't been here since the turn of the century. The original interior of mosaic tiled floor, tin walls and ceiling have been embellished with the addition of a large mahogany bar and intimate dining booths and tables. Victorian mirrors and old photos and paintings from the Korn's large private collection of memorabilia of "yesterday" adorn the walls, and antique stained-glass lamps and hanging plants complete the *fin de siecle* decor.

Richard and his wife Maria were the first cooks; now Maria is general manager, and Richard oversees the operation. They are most concerned that guests will feel comfortable at Yesterday's and find the service friendly; staff meetings are held three times a week to ensure that things run smoothly. Everything on the menu is "time tested" and the freshest ingredients possible are used—no preservatives or canned goods are permitted. The standing menu consists of a good selection of crisp salads, jumbo-sized hamburgers (½ lb. of choice ground beef, marinated and seasoned), interesting sandwiches and daily specials ranging from baked ham and beans, mussels Provencale, chicken Creole and beef stroganoff for lunch, to roast duck Normandy, scallops Florentine, baked trout with almonds and pineapple, and broiled swordfish for dinner. A blackboard crammed full of additional chef's specials ensures that there's bound to be something to appeal to every taste and pocket.

Appetizers and snacks are available at the bar as well the full menu. A recent addition of a bar and dining area forms a new entry way to the restaurant and here a different evening menu is served in slightly more sophisticated surroundings. Centrally located in downtown Newport, Yesterday's has a good reputation for serving excellent food in an informal and nostalgic atmosphere.

YESTERDAY'S
28 Washington Square, Newport • (401) 847-0116, 847-0125

OPEN: 11:00 am to 1:00 am seven
   days a week, all year
LUNCH: 11:00 am to 11:00 pm
DINNER: 5:00 to 11:00 pm.
SEATS: 160
CHILDREN'S PORTIONS:
available
SEPARATE BAR: open 11:00 am
   to 1:00 am (weekends until 2:00 am)
CREDIT CARDS: MasterCard, Visa
PARKING: ample street parking
RESERVATIONS: usually only
   necessary for large parties

Crabmeat Oriental

SERVES 4—6

3 cups cold cooked rice
½ lb. fresh mushrooms, sliced
1 cup thinly sliced waterchestnuts
1 cup finely-chopped green pepper
3 pimientos, finely cut
2 cups crabmeat
¼ cup chopped parsley
¼ cup chopped chives

Dressing:
1 cup olive oil
3 tablespoons soy sauce
3 tablespoons vinegar
½ teaspoon Tabasco
2 teaspoons Dijon mustard
Salad greens

Combine the rice, mushrooms, water chestnuts, green pepper, pimiento, crabmeat and herbs. Blend together the oil, soy sauce, vinegar, Tabasco and mustard. Pour the dressing over the salad mixture and toss well. Arrange on a bed of salad greens.

Filet of Sole Geraldine

SERVES 4

1½ lbs. filet of sole
1 lb. sliced fresh mushrooms
4 small scallions, diced
1 lb. tiny shrimp
8 oz. clarified butter
⅓ cup flour
4 eggs, beaten
3 oz. dry Vermouth
1 tablespoon fresh chopped parsley
4 lemon wedges
Salt and white pepper

Heat butter in saute pan, dust fish in flour and dip into beaten eggs. Saute lightly (approximately 2 minutes per side). Remove from pan and place on a warm plate. Add mushrooms, scallions and shrimp to pan. Saute until tender; drain excess butter from pan and flame with Vermouth. Add salt and pepper to taste and the chopped parsley. Spoon over fish and garnish with lemon wedges.

Chicken Cynthian
SERVES 4

4 8-oz. chicken breasts
4 slices of eggplant
4 oz. Prosciutto ham (4 slices)
1 lb. Parmesan cheese
1 cup flour
2 cups bread crumbs
4 eggs, beaten
1 pint hot tomato sauce
1 tablespoon oil

Remove skin from chicken breasts. Dust the chicken with flour. Beat eggs, dip the chicken breasts in egg and coat them with bread crumbs. Follow the same procedure with four slices of eggplant.

Heat a large skillet and add butter. Cook chicken breasts slowly for 4 minutes. Meanwhile fry the eggplant slices in oil in a small saute pan until golden brown on both sides. Turn the chicken breasts over and top each piece with one slice of eggplant, one slice of prosciutto ham and 4 oz. Parmesan cheese. Place in oven and bake for 10 minutes at 350 degrees. Take out and top with hot homemade tomato sauce.

Chicken Tarragon Stew
SERVES 6—8

3 lbs. boneless chicken meat, preferably breast
1½ lbs. sliced fresh mushrooms
1½ lbs. sliced onions
½ cup Chablis
1 cup heavy cream
½ cup flour
2 oz. vegetable oil
1 tablespoon tarragon leaves
1 tablespoon Worcestershire sauce
Salt and white pepper
1 tablespoon fresh chopped parsley

Cut chicken into bite-size pieces and dust them in flour. Heat oil in a small brasserie and saute chicken until all sides are seared. Add mushrooms, onions and tarragon to pan and saute until tender. Add white wine and simmer until liquid is reduced by half (about 6 to 8 minutes). Add cream and Worcestershire sauce and reduce again. Add salt and pepper to taste.

Serve over rice or egg noodles; top with chopped parsley.

Veal Monterey

SERVES 8

8 thin slices avocado
16 veal scallops, pounded thin (about 2 lbs.)
8 thin slices tomato, drained on paper towels
8 slices Monterey Jack cheese
8 tablespoons freshly grated Parmesan cheese
8 oz. tiny shrimp, cooked
Flour
2 eggs, beaten
2 cups breadcrumbs
2 to 4 tablespoons clarified butter
Salt and freshly-ground pepper
Lemon wedges for garnish

Place one avocado slice over one veal scallop. Top this with one tomato slice and one slice Monterey Jack cheese. Sprinkle with one tablespoon Parmesan cheese. Season with salt and pepper to taste. Top with 1 oz. shrimp. Cover with a second veal scallop. Pinch edges of veal together tightly to form a packet. Repeat with the remaining veal, avocado, tomato, cheese and shrimp. Refrigerate until firm, about 1 to 1½ hours.

Dust veal with flour. Shake off excess and dip into beaten egg. Then roll in bread crumbs, covering the veal completely. Heat butter in a large skillet over medium high heat. Add veal to skillet in batches (do not over-crowd) and saute until lightly browned, about three to five minutes per side. Transfer veal to serving platter and garnish with lemon wedges.

CAFE ZELDA

Cafe Zelda, a favorite local haunt hidden away on Lower Thames Street, has recently been taken over by new owner Thomas "Cal" Callahan. Formerly the bar tender at Zelda's for six years, Cal has chosen not to rename the restaurant, and has in fact changed little about this popular bistro, apart from filling the walls with his collection of dramatic original prints of America's Cup races and famous sailing vessels, adding a nautical flavor to the stylish decor.

Formerly a brewery, this old corner building was more recently the site of McGee's, a local bar in what was then the 5th ward. Zelda's still has a strong neighborhood clientele, essential for year-round survival in a summer resort.

Two chefs take turns in preparing the food at Zelda's. The menu is comprehensive and carefully selected to ensure there's something for everyone, from fresh seafood to steaks, chicken and veal. Special entrees and appetizers are available each day depending on the Chef's whim—could be brook trout *meuniere*, pan-blackened mako shark, or steamed littleneck clams in garlic oil. Specialties are smoked mussels in a cream Dijon sauce (as requested by *Gourmet* magazine), fried calamari, and shrimp Italiano (see following recipe). Prices are reasonable, the service straightforward, the atmosphere cosmopolitan. A small but adequate wine list complements the menu.

The lunch menu consists of soups, appetizers, sandwiches, salads and varied specialties including pasta and seafood dishes. And let's not forget the Zelda Burger, topped with melted Swiss, sauteed mushrooms, onion, and tomato.

The narrow, L-shaped dining room on two levels has been cleverly designed to allow intimate dining at tables tucked away in corners or behind half-walls. Original varnished oak paneling and woodwork is much in evidence and offset by soft carpeting and subdued lighting from period wall sconces. Lace curtains frame the full-length windows, shaded by green awnings, which look out onto the street. Table settings are elegant with an abundance of crisp white linen. The separate bar, through which one enters, offers room to eat and enjoy the full menu in a pub-like atmosphere.

All in all, Cafe Zelda, just a short walk down Thames Street from town center, is a great little place to know about.

CAFE ZELDA
528 Thames Street, Newport • (401) 849-4002

OPEN: every day, all year
LUNCH: 11:30 am—2:30 pm, Monday through Saturday
DINNER: 5:30—10 pm, Sunday through Thursday,
        5:30 — 11:00 Friday and Saturday
SUNDAY BRUNCH: 12 am—3 pm
SEPARATE BAR: open until 1:00 am
SEATS: 47
CHILDREN'S PORTIONS: not available
CREDIT CARDS: AMEX, CB, DC, MC, VISA
PARKING: usually ample off-street parking
RESERVATIONS: advised — call 849-4002

Calamari Aioli

1½ lbs. calamari (squid) tubes
8 whole garlic cloves
6 egg yolks
2 teaspoons minced garlic
2¼ cups olive oil
½ teaspoon cayenne pepper
3 oz. lemon juice
salt and white pepper to taste

Rinse calamari well in cold water and slice tubes into small rings.

Place garlic cloves and two tablespoons olive oil in a small pie tin. Cover with foil and bake in oven at 375 degrees until cloves are soft and brown (20 to 25 minutes). Remove and roughly chop the garlic cloves.

Place egg yolks, lemon juice and raw minced garlic in a mixer. Beat on high until yolks have reached the ribbon stage, approximately 5 to 7 minutes. Add roasted garlic. Drizzle the remaining olive oil into mixer in a slow steady stream while mixer is running until it is all incorporated. Remove the aioli from the bowl and season with cayenne pepper, salt and white pepper, and refrigerate.

Dust calamari with seasoned flour, shaking off the excess. Deep fry in vegetable oil for just 35 to 45 seconds, until crisp and brown. Remove and drain excess oil. Serve on a warm oval platter with aioli and a large lemon wedge.

Smoked Mussels in Mustard-Cream Sauce

1 teaspoon minced scallion greens
1 teaspoon minced garlic
½ cup freshly smoked mussels
    (available at some specialty foods shops,
    or substitute canned)
1 tablespoon clarified butter
1 teaspoon Dijon-style mustard
1 teaspoon coarse-grained mustard
2 tablespoons dry white wine
¼ cup heavy cream
1 tablespoon minced fresh parsley

In a skillet cook the scallion, garlic and mussels in butter over moderate heat, shaking the skillet gently, for one minute. Add the mustards, wine and cream and cook the mixture, stirring gently, until it comes to a bare simmer. Spoon the mixture onto 2 heated plates and sprinkle the parsley over it. Serves 2 as a first course.

Scampi Italiano
SERVES 2

10 U-15 shrimp, peeled
2 tablespoons olive oil
3 tablespoons garlic, chopped
1 tablespoon shallots, chopped
2 tablespoons tomatoes, chopped
½ teaspoon each fresh basil, thyme
**   and oregano, chopped**
1 package fresh spinach
2 tablespoons unsalted butter
½ cup white wine
salt and white pepper

Saute shrimp briefly in olive oil, remove from heat and keep warm. Add garlic, shallots, tomatoes and fresh herbs to the pan. Saute for one minute and deglaze with ¼ cup white wine. Reduce wine, remove from heat and whisk in the butter.

    Wash spinach leaves thoroughly and poach them lightly in the remaining wine in a separate pan. Quickly remove from pan and arrange in a circle on each warm plate. Add shrimp to sauce and heat through. Spoon the scampi into the spinach circles and serve.

Grilled Yellow Fin Tuna with Ginger Wasabi Beurre Blanc SERVES 2

2 8-oz. yellow fin tuna steaks
¼ cup white wine
3 tablespoons fresh ginger, grated
2 tablespoons shallots, chopped
3 oz. heavy cream
1 lb. unsalted butter
1 tablespoon wasabi powder
salt and white pepper

Reduce white wine with shallots and grated ginger in a copper pot. Add heavy cream and reduce again. Remove pan from flame and slowly whisk in butter. Add wasabi powder and season with salt and white pepper. Grill tuna steaks on high heat for 2 or 3 minutes (medium rare). Serve on heated plates topped with the sauce.

Chicken with Fine Herbes and Sundried Tomatoes SERVES 2

2 8-oz. boneless chicken breasts, cut into julienne strips
10 sundried tomatoes cut julienne
½ teaspoon each freshly-chopped basil,
    thyme and tarragon
2 tablespoons olive oil
2 tablespoons shallots, chopped
¼ cup heavy cream
¼ cup white wine
salt and white pepper to taste
½ lb. fettucine, cooked al dente
¼ cup parmesan cheese

Saute sundried tomatoes and shallots in olive oil in a skillet for a few minutes. Add chicken, cook on both sides until almost done, then deglaze the pan with white wine. Add the fresh herbs, heavy cream and pasta. Reduce the heavy cream over medium heat while tossing the pasta gently. Season with salt and white pepper. Garnish with chopped parsley and parmesan cheese.

Baked Apple Tartine

1½ lbs. Granny Smith apples
2 cups flour
pinch of salt
½ cup butter
¼ cup brown sugar
½ teaspoon ground cinnamon
¼ teaspoon grated nutmeg
¼ teaspoon ground cloves
⅓ cup golden raisins

Preheat oven to 400 degrees. Sift flour and salt together into a bowl and rub in the butter. Add ice-cold water slowly, enough to mix to a firm dough.

Peel, core and slice the apples into a bowl. Add brown sugar, spices and raisins. Put mixture into a buttered deep 1 quart pie dish. Sprinkle 2 tablespoons water over the apples.

Roll out dough and cover the pie. Decorate the crust with dough trimmings. Brush with milk and sprinkle with a tablespoon of granulated sugar.

Bake for 20 minutes at 400 degrees. Reduce heat to 350 degrees and continue to bake for another 20 minutes. Serve warm with a scoop of ice cream or fresh whipped cream.

INDEX

BOOK ORDER FORM

Quantity	Title	Amount
_____	A TASTE OF NEWPORT @ $7.50	_____
_____	A TASTE OF PROVIDENCE @ $7.50	_____
_____	A TASTE OF CAPE COD @ $7.50	_____
_____	A TASTE OF PROVINCETOWN @ $7.50	_____
_____	THE BARONS OF NEWPORT @ $7.50	_____
_____	COMPLETE GUIDE TO NEWPORT @ $5.95	_____
_____	TRADITIONAL PORTUGUESE RECIPES FROM PROVINCETOWN @ $7.50	_____
_____	THE PROVINCETOWN ARTISTS COOKBOOK @ $9.95	_____

TOTAL: _____

*Shipping: _____

TOTAL AMOUNT: _____

*Please add $2.00 for each book and $1.25 for each additional book for handling and shipping charges. For orders of two or more books, please give street address so we can ship UPS.

Make checks payable to:

SHANK PAINTER PUBLISHING CO.
650 Commercial Street
Provincetown, MA 02657

(508) 487-9169